THINKING
ALLOWED

A Teenager's View on Human Rights

Sun Young Hwang

PARTRIDGE
A Penguin Random House Company

ISBN: Hardcover   978-1-4828-9758-6
               Softcover   978-1-4828-9757-9
               eBook   978-1-4828-9759-3

To order additional copies of this book, contact
Toll Free 800 101 2657 (Singapore)
Toll Free 1 800 81 7340 (Malaysia)
orders.singapore@partridgepublishing.com

www.partridgepublishing.com/singapore

TABLE OF CONTENTS

Part IV: Human Rights in Korea

Part V: Human Rights through Education

PROLOGUE

I n elementary school, I would run out onto the playground every recess to play with my friends. I would suggest new games, gather more kids around me, and make hilarious jokes. However back in the classroom, I would be the shy girl again sitting in the window seat who always listened attentively and quietly to the teacher, taking notes on every word. It was strange and even ironic how I found it particularly difficult to think differently and actively when I was in the classroom than when I was on the playground at recess.

After I graduated from elementary school and became a middle school student, I still sat in the window seat, but this time I felt different. I listened to the many lectures of course, but I also stared out the window and came to believe that there must be more outside than just what we learned from our textbooks inside school. And although I still took notes with a pencil of every word the teacher told us, I found myself faintly scribbling down my own thoughts right next to the teacher's. Sometimes the scribbles would be simply additional questions I wanted to research, but many other times, the scribbles would be my opinions which sometimes did differ from my teacher's. My first attempt at critical and deep thinking started 6 years ago, at the window seat.

As a high school student, I was fortunate enough to study a vast range of subjects and participate in different kinds of activities. However the three that intrigued me most and helped me most were debating, philosophy, and human rights. If debating taught me to think critically and how to question authority and assumptions, studying philosophy taught me to take a step back and think more deeply and ponder the details of fundamental issues. Human rights taught me to expand my thoughts to others and think with both distinct value and passion.

Although I am still a teenager in years with much more to learn, if high school taught me one thing, it was that "thinking" must always be allowed and indeed cherished. Living in Korea, I feel that, despite the many excellent qualities we have as a nation, the current education system is not very think-friendly for students. That is, many students still repeat the routine of staring at the blackboard, listening to lectures, taking notes, and memorizing them. I believe that if education aims to maximize our potential and create new possibilities, thinking should be allowed and expanded in both depth and breadth. Thinking should also be "aloud." We should actively express our thoughts verbally, and society should listen to look for a way to reflect our opinions and create a genuine consensus.

My book is my personal attempt to think aloud about what I believe is important to me. More specifically, this book is an introduction to certain human right issues within Korea, but with the perspective of a teenager of course, and with a more philosophical foundation. When I had the fortunate opportunity to take an online college course called "Human Rights: A Philosophical Introduction," I realized how meaningful it would be to look at the philosophy driving the different human right issues in Korea. The first sections of my book introduce, explain, and discuss the necessary philosophical concepts that will be dealt with later in terms of specific human rights issues in Korea. My plan is to have this book be an introductory manual to creating a fresh lens for looking at human rights and the issues that are important to explore and examine that relate to those rights.

PART I

THE FOUNDATIONS AND CHALLENGES

WHERE DO HUMAN RIGHTS COME FROM?

When young kids ask their parents what babies are, the question is not so hard to answer. Most parents would be able to provide an eloquent explanation. However, when a kid blinks innocently and asks, "Where do babies come from?" or "How are babies made?," many parents might gulp and laugh uneasily. Amusingly, many Korean parents lie to their kids by saying that storks drop babies from the sky or that, if they hold hands and sleep, a baby is born the next morning.

Similarly, the question "What are human rights?" is not that difficult to answer. Although no absolute consensus exists on the specifics, in general human rights are explained as rights inherent to human beings to which we are entitled to without discrimination. They are "inalienable," "indivisible," and "universal" rights accompanied by many other powerful qualities.

However the question "Where do human rights come from?" might leave us quite dumbfounded. Indeed, where do we get those impressive, grand presents that are surprisingly "free" for everyone—as long as they are human beings? This uncertainty is one of the reasons why it is meaningful to examine more closely the various attempts that have been made to find the philosophical foundation for the notion of human rights. With this exact inquiry, I enrolled in Professor Mathias

Risse's Harvard Extension School course entitled Human Rights—A Philosophical Introduction, which not only provided an enriching chance to learn about the major approaches to the foundation of human rights but also triggered me to apply such knowledge to other branches of study. In this essay, I would like to briefly introduce the three approaches I learned in Professor Risse's lectures and discuss their differences.

The first and probably most common approach is the natural rights approach, which states that human rights are certain rights that we had in our "natural" state before any government was established. These rights existed by nature—that is, they are part of the infrastructure of nature and are independent of human design, activities, or human mind and reason. Such natural rights can, like the natural laws of physics, be observed and realized.

The second more complicated approached is the Kantian self-consistency approach, which establishes the concept of human rights through a logical process of thought. Immanuel Kant identified the source of all values as our own rational nature. He stated that, as rational agents, we are committed to value ourselves in order to confer value to the course of the actions we choose. By extending the scope to include other people as well, Kant demonstrated that every other individual also has a rational nature and, thus, values him—or herself for the same reason. This leads to the conclusion that, if I undermine another person and treat him/her "merely as a means," I would be equally degrading my own capacity, which would be a contradiction with my own commitment to value myself as an agent. Therefore, through self-consistency, Kant demonstrated the establishment of universal human rights.

The final and most recently developed approach to proving human rights comes from a modern American-born philosopher, James Griffin. Griffin introduced the concept of reasonable acceptability as an alternative to explain the establishment of human rights. According to Griffin, we must find living arrangements that are reasonably acceptable to every single person. With this, he elaborated upon the human status and what a distinctively human life is. Thus, there are certain necessary qualities that allow us to actually make our position in the world and create our lives uniquely as a normative agent. The sources of rights that come from personhood, as enumerated by Griffin, are autonomy, minimal provisions, and liberty. Griffin claimed that human rights were established to protect any one of these three elements that qualify us as a normative agent.

The basic difference among these approaches is that they derive human rights from different sources. More specifically, the natural rights method relies on the existence of God to account for the justification of fundamental rights and moral equality, arguing that we were all created in the image of God and such similarities are more significant than the subtle differences. However, due to this trait, the natural rights approach has failed to become a foundation for universal human rights as it depends on a particular theology.

Kant's argument and Griffin's argument are similar in the sense that they have sources that appear to be universal—rational nature for Kant and the distinctive human existence for Griffin—but are distinguished in the sense that Kant further develops his view with the notion of the famous categorical imperative, which essentially grants certain absolute rights to rational beings. Indeed, although Kant and Griffin shared the view on the importance of dignity, Kant claimed that dignity is inviolable and we can never forfeit or waive it; it is inherently inalienable. On the contrary, Griffin stated that, although the standards for the violation of dignity are high, it is not categorically or absolutely inviolable.

Of these three approaches, my personal preference is for the Kantian self-consistency foundation primarily because the other approaches, although meaningful, do not provide a foundation for absolute rights. One might argue that there are no absolute rights in the first place. However, a distinction must be made between having an intrinsic, undeniable right and then reluctantly compromising it due to the realistic limitations and having a right that is, by its nature, susceptible to adjustment according to circumstances.

Kant's establishment of human rights is frequently criticized for its unreasonably high demand. A rigid, strict theory based on self-consistency could seem overly demanding. However, to defend Kant, the reason why we perceive his approach to be unrealistic and not feasible is because we are not just comprised of a rational nature that he so heavily emphasizes. Rather, we have irrationality and emotion along with pure rationality; consequently, Kant's doctrine seems to be overly exhausting. However, the unique significance of Kant's approach is that, although rationality might not be the entirety of our nature, it is our defining character. In other words, rationality is what defines us uniquely and distinctively as human beings. Thus, it does not seem so strange to explain and prove the existence of human rights by emphasizing pure rationality.

However, I would further propose that, as people are not just rational beings and we are moved greatly by emotions as well, the extension and promotion of human rights should not rely exclusively on the Kantian model. In order to make human rights seem more intuitively plausible, we should appeal to other faculties inherent within people, such as sympathy and compassion. To conclude, the existence of human rights could be relatively well explained by the Kantian model, but the promotion of human rights could be done in collaboration with more emphasis on emotional sympathy and compassion for others.

The philosophical foundation for human rights is not just a part of history; it is a continual intellectual quest. I believe that one of the reasons why it is extremely hard to eradicate the countless human rights abuses worldwide is because we are still struggling to define a concrete explanation that refutes and stands against such challenges. Tragedies such as the Norway massacre continue because there are still individuals who sincerely and entirely do not understand why all people should be equally entitled with inherent and inviolable rights. We must strive to find a more fundamental answer that could refute and prevent people such as that far-right terrorist who mercilessly killed 77 people in Norway and released a 1,500-page manifesto justifying and elaborating upon extreme nationalistic views that blatantly override the principle of universal human rights.

Where do human rights come from?

My own answer is quite simple. Human rights ultimately come from our unwavering and vigorous effort to achieve a better world in which every person—regardless of nationality, gender, ethnicity, color, language, religion, or any other status—is genuinely and fully respected.

AN ANSWER TO A SKEPTIC

"The path of sound credence is through the thick forest of skepticism"
George Jean Nathan

The fact that some people are skeptical of the idea of human rights is not surprising at all. In fact, as difficult and complicated as it is to prove the foundation of human rights, it is just as easy to poke holes at the notions of fundamental and universal entitlements granted to every single individual. However as George Jean Nathan said, the "thick forest of skepticism" is a necessary path that must be endured in order to add more confidence and weight to the ideal one is seeking to achieve. Thus, in this short essay, I would like to briefly introduce the several different types of skeptics I encountered in Professor Risse's lectures.

The first skeptic, John Stuart Mill, can be considered a critic of human rights because he essentially argued that rights should not be basic. According to Mill, rights are the best devices for social coordination, but when they are not adequately used to maximize happiness, they can and should be set aside.

A refutation to John Stuart Mill could be that his theory, utilitarianism, is essentially one that throws out too much of the protection of human rights. In other words, if utilitarianists do not

6

take the protection of individuals as something basic and fundamental, they will have to confront circumstances in which some people are sacrificing and losing too much to the extent that it is grievously problematic.

A typical example of this observable fact would be the sheriff example: According to pure utilitarianism thinking, a sheriff might have to turn over an innocent man to an angry mob in order to protect himself, satisfy and maximize the town's utility, and avoid a resulting riot. Likewise, the blind abidance to a utilitarian calculation of utility could lead to a gross denial of even the most minimum level of rights and dignity for each individual. This massive sacrifice demonstrates the structural, systematic weakness of Utilitarianism and points to the fact that not only must there be limits to a consequentialist viewpoint, but we must also be motivated to look for an alternative that takes each person seriously.

Another famous skeptic, Nietzsche, rejected the fundamental idea of moral equality. He claimed that, in the initial state of human history, no such concept of equality existed; rather, there were those in power and those who were governed. According to Nietzsche, the influence of Christianity deluded the weaker people in society to believe that they in fact were important members and that moral equality existed. Ultimately, Nietzsche criticized human rights by saying that, without the lies of theology, there is no way to prove the existence of moral equality.

To Nietzsche, we could present the ideas of philosophers such as James Griffin, who argued that mere personhood—or the fact that we simply have the traits of a distinctively human life—is what provides fundamental moral equality. We could add that, in fact, historical attempts to find a non-universal morality or justify discriminatory theories have thus far failed. It only requires a peek into history to see how feeble the efforts have been in arguing for a morality that singles out particular people for special status. Efforts to back such relativist thought have not met with much intellectual success, and in every developed culture some kind of universal reflection has occurred.

The next skeptic is Michael J. Perry, who argued that human rights must ineliminably go together with Christianity. This viewpoint is in stark contrast from the universal concept of human rights, which is not dependent on theology or certain political ideologies. Perry challenges us to find a non-parochial justification of human rights.

To Perry, one refutation could be that we do not necessarily need the notion of absolute sacredness of rights; in such a case, we do not necessarily need any religious element either. There are in fact secular, non-parochial justifications for human rights, such as the Kantian self-consistency approach or James Griffin's reasonable acceptability approach, which find the source of human rights not from theology, but from rational nature and distinctive human existence, respectively.

Although clearly not a skeptic, Griffin also expressed some concerns for the status and situation of human rights talk in the current century. More specifically, Griffin advocated for a more limited scope of the concept of human rights—mainly due to his concern that the prevalence of human rights talk would eventually degrade the importance of such rights. He would rather keep the language and names properly aligned with specifically the moral problems. Griffin's standard of judging which rights pertain to the scope of human rights was based on whether those rights are necessary to protect the distinct human status of being a normative agency. In other words, human rights are not concerned with the issue of simply enhancing human good and flourishing, but rather with defending and maintaining the distinctive human existence and human status. Specifically, he highlighted three sources of rights derived from personhood—autonomy, minimal provisions, and liberty—and declared that rights protecting any one of these three elements are to be considered human rights.

Some major examples of those who fall outside the scope of human rights under Griffin's standards are children and sexual minorities (lesbian, gay, bisexual, transgender). Griffin did not state that we can treat those who do not fall under the scope of human rights in any way we please. Rather, he assigned alternative rights for those groups. In the case of sexual minorities, for example, Griffin argued that their particular legal rights should be considered as civil and political rights rather than human rights. However, Griffin did seem to prioritize human rights over these alternative rights.

My personal evaluation of Griffin's limited scope is that it is quite arbitrary and does not render the notion of human rights to be more determinate. It could be considered quite arbitrary in the sense that the qualities that protect the unique human status could be aligned with the different rights, like civil and political rights. The example of sexual minorities' rights could be assigned as rights that protect Griffin's definition of liberty—namely, the quality that ensures that others will not be able to forcibly stop someone from pursuing what he/she values in life. If a gay couple desires to marry because that is what they mutually value in life, they might demand liberty to ensure that others do not forcibly stop them from pursuing their marriage. Likewise, the boundaries are so thin and subjective that the limited scope will just be symbolic, without being practically useful.

Another reason why I disagree with Griffin's limited scope is that his premise—when an issue becomes prevalent it will lose value and get "flogged"—is not necessarily correct. Such a premise only pertains to goods that are valuable because of their rarity; for such goods, the increase of quantity could directly lead to the degrading of their value. However human rights are not valuable because they are rare and given to only exclusive groups. They have their intrinsic value; in fact, this value becomes more worthy when elevated to a universal value that everyone tries to uphold.

Finally, I believe that if we divide rights into small sectors and exclude them from the dominant human rights movement, those who are excluded will become minorities once again. In other words, the reason why sexual minorities and children could be blessed with increasing rights in the current century is probably because they were incorporated into the mainstream wave for the promotion of general human rights. If those rights are to stand on a separate island once more, they will be too conveniently reduced to something insignificant.

The last type of skeptic I would like to discuss is the one who thinks that people do not have any other rights than the legal rights guaranteed by the constitution and laws of the country in which they respectively live. I question the legitimacy of such an opponent: What legitimacy do they themselves have to say that the constitution and national laws become the supreme law of human beings? If we are born in that nation and do not have the option to move out of that land due to physical barriers, which is typical for most people, does the territory in which we are born decide what kind of basic rights we have?

Obviously, the refutations discussed in this short essay would not be sufficient to tackle the long history of skepticism. However, engaging in critical thinking to tackle the philosophy of those who think differently is a meaningful and challenging intellectual activity in itself. Although the notion of human rights has always been in dispute, as can be observed from the increased number of individuals devoting their lives to help others, the undeniable fact is that this intellectual debate is helping our credence grow stronger, not weaker.

ARE HUMAN RIGHTS UNAVOIDABLY RELIGIOUS?

An important challenge to the philosophical foundation of human rights involves the fundamental skepticism: "Where do we get these rights from? Do they just drop from the sky? Or are they artificially made?" To this, several philosophers, such as Michael J. Perry, have argued that human rights must come from theology or that the crucial element of the sacredness of human rights can only be proved with the element of religion. Other philosophers—most famously the modern philosopher Ronald Dworkin—have disagreed with Perry's idea of ineliminably religious human rights.

This essay was written after reading Perry's well-known article entitled "Is the Idea of Human Rights Ineliminably Religious?" This essay analyzes Perry's thesis and main argument, but also offers some refutations to his thoughts. More specifically, the essay discusses my own rebuttals, some possible refutations that Dworkin might have made to Perry's analysis, and also what Perry could have said to such objections.

In his insightful article entitled "Is the Idea of Human Rights Ineliminably Religious?" Michael J. Perry claimed that the concept of human rights is inescapably religious as there cannot be an intellectual, secular explanation that decisively proves the sacredness of each and every human being. He carefully developed his argument based on

11

two explicit premises: (1) The crucial foundation of human rights is the conviction that all human beings are sacred and (2) the concept of sacredness is ineliminably religious. From these two consecutive propositions, Perry concluded that human rights can only be explained in a religious sense.

Perry introduced his first premise by stating that his predominant interest in one constituent of the idea of human rights, which is "a foundational one: the conviction that every human being is sacred." The obscure notion of sacredness is then defined in more specific terms, such as inherent dignity and worth, inviolable, and being an end in itself. To clarify, to say that every human being is sacred is essentially to argue that human beings—just because they are human beings—have an intrinsic value that cannot be trampled on. This inborn sacrosanctity is what entitles all people to fundamental rights: "[C]ertain things ought not to be done to any human being and certain other things ought to be done for every human being."

This first premise contributes to the overall argument by offering the burden that the secular version of human rights must fulfill. In other words, the nonreligious explanation should not merely account for why human beings have worth. It must also extend the discussion and prove why every person is valuable to the extent of being uninfringeable.

However, whether the premise best supports the article's main argument is questionable. Frankly speaking, the notion that human beings are sacred and inviolable is not as absolute as Perry claimed. Moreover, the notion carries a fairly minor impact because it is impossible to materialize in reality. Human beings cannot remain so sacrosanct and unbreakable. In fact, even when we are trying to uphold someone's crucial rights, we could be infringing on his/her other aspects. When we ban abortion for the sake of protecting the right to life, for example, we might be trespassing upon mothers' right to choose. Likewise, although the idea of sacrosanctity could serve as a good sound bite, it does not have much feasibility or impact and thus does not support the argument sufficiently.

The second premise of Perry's argument is that the discussion of sacredness is ineliminably religious. Perry further elucidated that a religious conviction is one that is embedded in faith that the world is genuinely meaningful in a deeply intimate way. Such religious discussion would surround the fundamental questions of how one is linked with others, the world, and an ultimate reality. Thus, the nature of religion itself invites individuals to value the connections with others.

In Christianity, for example, Jesus commands us to love our neighbors and enemies alike; Buddhism similarly calls for compassion to for all living things. Perry explicitly pointed out that "the experience of all human beings as sacred is widely shared among different sects and religious . . . and that common ground helps explain the emergence of the idea of human rights as a point of convergence among peoples from different religious traditions." He then questioned whether the morality in an agnostic framework—which usually views the world as being void of meaning—can be comparable to the morality in a religious framework in which the world is deeply connected and meaningful.

The second premise plays the role of making a clear distinction between what is religious and nonreligious, consequently stressing the uniqueness of the former. It sheds light on the inevitable relationship among human rights, morality, and religion, thereby clarifying the direction of the overall argument. However, the link that Perry emphasized between sacredness and religion is actually quite disputed when we see how religion itself—in both the use and content of the Scriptures—frequently invites violation of the most fundamental dignity of human beings. Sandra Schneider's "Does the Bible Have a Postmodern Message?" revealed the various violations and abuses that stem from the content and usage of the Scriptures. When the Qur'an states that men can beat women, clerics say that homosexuals should be thrown off a mountain or stoned to death, and the Catholic Church commits child abuse, the so-called ineliminably durable association between sacrosanctity of human beings and religion is undermined.

To Perry's argument on human rights being inescapably religious, Ronald Dworkin expressed a different viewpoint: The sacredness of every human being is not a religious tenet, but a "secular and deep philosophical belief." Dworkin argued that we value human beings not because of religion, but because of their unique eminence among all natural creations and because of their embodiment of the accumulated years of process to become more multi-faceted, cultured, and developed. In other words, human beings have intrinsic and objective value because in each and every person there is an unprecedented amount of investment coming from various sources.

The second counter-argument that Dworkin made to Perry is that human rights can still be explained even when the world is not as ultimately meaningful as the religious sense demands it to be. Although the whole world does not have a personally binding significance, we can still assign importance to a variety of specific human activities. This view is very convincing: In reality, we do not perceive every single component of the world as critically meaningful and intimate; rather, we place the greater focus and value on certain areas that we cannot give up on or must celebrate. This selection of certain activities that require more attention actually grants them a greater opportunity to be valued than simply choosing to look at the macroscopic significance of the whole world.

A final refutation that Dworkin could make is that the religious version of explaining human rights lacks universality. Although the concept of sacredness and morality can be discussed in a religious framework, it cannot extend to those who are nonreligious and agnostic. That is, the religious version that links rights to God inevitably excludes those who do not believe in the existence of the latter. However the secular discussion of human rights does not actively exclude certain groups as it is a form of rational reasoning that does not require concessions to spiritual elements. Therefore the secular version holds more potential to be adopted for the conception of universal morality and universal human rights.

To the series of objections above, Perry might respond by saying that Dworkin's claim goes against the very spirit of human rights because it requires certain elements from people in order for them to be valued. Perry would say it is not because of the multiple investments and creative energy that human beings are to be thought of as sacred; rather, they are to be respected simply because they are human beings. Dworkin's reasoning implies that, without the various inputs such as parental care or the evolutionary process, human beings are not important at all. Perry would also find Dworkin's claim of only certain human activities being valuable problematic. The selectiveness itself could be a unique source of abuse as it would invite arbitrary standards of what is deemed important and what is not. Moreover, it could arouse conflicts over the different opinions regarding how to prioritize the more "valuable" human activities.

ARE HUMAN BEINGS REALLY THAT UNIQUE?

Another challenge in establishing the philosophical foundation of human rights is the issue of whether the rights to which we are entitled are inherently limited to human beings. What makes human beings so unique? What about animal rights? One of the most famous philosophers who argued that the line between human beings and animals is arbitrary when regarding the rights to which they are entitled is Peter Singer. In his insightful writing "Animal Liberation," Singer took a step forward and argued for animal rights.'

The following essay is an attempt to analyze Singer's thoughts and offer some refutations or suggestions to them. It is based on the essay I submitted to the 20th International Philosophy Olympiad held in Oslo, Norway. In the International Philosophy Olympiad, students are required to choose from one of the four given quotations and write an essay for four hours (without any external research materials provided), philosophically analyzing and expanding the quotation of their choice.

"If (an animal) suffers, there can be no moral justification for disregarding that suffering, or for refusing to count it equally with the like suffering of any other being. But the converse of this is also true. If a being is not capable of

suffering, or of enjoyment, there is nothing to take into account."

Peter Singer, *Animal Liberation*

Throughout history, we have encountered several waves of demands for emancipation. The long struggle of the anti-slavery movement was followed by the call for women's rights and more recently the surge for protection of minors. However the flourishing of such a human rights culture has been criticized for having been an unconscious process of select and focus—selecting and romanticizing the human race while neglecting and disregarding other animal species. Although the concept of animal liberation has been  belittled and even scoffed at, the importance of making a philosophical examination of this issue becomes clear when we observe the blatant abuses condoned in almost every industry that deals with animals. The core reason why chickens are caged without seeing any sunlight for their entire lifespan and fattened to the extremity that their legs break stems from the lack of fundamental respect for animals as a whole.

In this essay, I hope to dive into the crux of this philosophical debate while raising additional critical questions to consider. I will first analyze the given quotation by Peter Singer, simultaneously questioning its validity. I then plan to reveal the important premises of the theory of animal liberation to demonstrate that there is indeed a distinct and differentiated value for specifically human beings. Finally, I will present a more personal evaluation of the issue.

It is easy to profess one's concern for the welfare of animals. However, the real dilemma boils down to the extent of such concern. Singer takes a rather bold stance by arguing that there is no "moral justification" for "disregarding" the suffering of animals. By this, he is essentially arguing not for a simplistic love for animals, but for the establishment of animal rights. That is, to state that it is immoral for us to neglect the pain that animals feel is to say that we must actually take an action to put an end to such suffering. Thus, animals can demand us of certain modes of treatment and we have no moral justification to stand still, neglecting their calls. In this way, Singer touched upon the essential element that constitutes a right: the ability of an entity to make a legitimate demand of others for a course of action.

Along with the request for animal rights, Singer made an additional move to suggest that animals and human beings are no different from their entitlement to a right if they feel the same amount of suffering. In fact, he argued that, if a person is not capable of suffering or of enjoyment, "there is nothing to take into account." Thus, his ultimate standard for who receives the general right to demand protection from others is the ability to feel suffering and enjoyment. However, this standard must answer several questions to be valid.

The first question regards the vagueness of the concepts of both suffering and enjoyment. Despite the fact that a long list of prominent philosophers have failed to reach a consistent agreement on what defines or constitutes pleasure and pain, Singer's simplistic concept is met with the inevitable vulnerability of how to measure such feelings. This is problematic when we consider that in reality there can be no "absolute rights" (for example, if abortion is legalized in order to uphold the rights of women's choice, this would undoubtedly bring up the issue of the fetus's right to life) and there must be prioritization of which rights are more significant than others. Such prioritization calls for a more sophisticated way of measuring the shades of difference in what is more suffering and what is the higher sort of enjoyment. Which would be more painful: a bird caged whose wings are removed or a woman who is raped and mentally distraught by the experience? Singer would have to provide a convincing hierarchy of the intensity of suffering and enjoyment in order for his argument to be considered more seriously.

Even if we assume that there is a concise, definite way of measuring Singer's standards, there still lingers the more fundamental doubt as to why the faculty of sensing pain and pleasure must be the ultimate standard. We see people volunteering to suffer through pain to make themselves stronger while others intentionally block their desires for earthly pleasures for various purposes. Yet even if we endure a reasonable amount of suffering and absence of happiness, we are still categorized as human beings entitled to the same rights. Thus, the question arises: Is Singer's standard proven significant enough to stand as the criteria for judging who has fundamental rights? To apply a more relevant context, just because students like us suffer from a massive workload and stress, are we automatically assigned to have rights over the protection of such pain? The better standard for establishing rights seems to be a more comprehensive one that incorporates other qualities of human beings or animals.

To take a step back from the various technical matters of this philosophical debate, it seems meaningful to examine the most important elephant in the room that is frequently taken for granted. The underlying premise behind any kind of rights discussion is the question of whether rights exist in the first place. From where do we—humans and animals alike—get rights? Are they granted from our creation or did we somehow artificially make them out of necessity?  Can there be a right-based morality? A more relevant question to this specific issue of animal liberation would be whether there could be a foundation of human rights that could equally apply to animals.

Although the justification of rights seems to be intuitively obvious, philosophers have struggled with its complexities. John Locke produced fresh insights into how we are bestowed with "natural rights" even before any state or government was institutionalized. However, this attempt (along with many others) relied on the existence of religion and God to prove the existence of rights. To briefly present the religious view, every being is a creation and thus an embodiment of God, meaning that we all have the obligation to care for each other as equal children of God. Human rights in a religious framework remain relatively untouched due to the fact that the existence of God cannot be conclusively proved or disproved.

Likewise, in the case of animal rights, this sort of religious foundation may be possible—namely, if there is a religion that clearly calls for the inherent value of specifically animals, then we could possibly say that the foundation is sufficient. (For example, both Hindu and Islamic religious tenets hold that certain animals such as cows or pigs are sacred and from that sense those animals are granted significant rights.) Therefore the religious justification of rights does not—in principle—prove that human beings are distinctively different from animals.

However the foundation in a religious framework is inevitably vulnerable as it cannot serve as a universal truth. If the legitimacy of rights depends on the words of God, this belief will only extend to those who have faith in the existence of that God. This is problematic when we consider that the nature of rights is to be able to demand of others a certain course of actions; no matter how vigorously a religious individual urges an agnostic neighbor to love others and care for them, the neighbor could quite conveniently shove off the request. This is why there have been additional attempts to seek a more secular version of justifying the existence of rights.

One of those attempts has been the idea of common goods: There are certain elements that we absolutely must have in life and that dire necessity itself is what creates rights for those elements. Some of those goods include the need for a reasonable level of health, education, wealth, or even a minimum level of dignity through acknowledgment by the society. Under this secular argument, there is room for people to argue that animals desire and need the same common goods. People could easily argue that animals need a minimum level of material goods and also point to the fact that animals have a sophisticated system of society, thereby proving the need for other social goods as well. Thus, this secular justification of rights also fails to prove that human beings are distinctively different from animals.

The secular version that does create a difference between animals and humans, thereby serving as a significant blow to the animal liberation theory, is the morality that Kant created with his stress on the importance of rationality. Kant argued that rational beings are characterized by their deliberate will to commit themselves to a certain course of actions. This will is different from the simple inclination or instinct to do that action. By taking an action, this rational being is essentially implying that the action has a value or a meaningful element. However, in order to confer a value to another action, the subject must have a reasonable value as well. As such, by choosing to act, we are actually committed to hold a value in ourselves as actors. Kant explained that this value in every rational being comes from the faculty of rationality that made that will possible. As this value exists in all rational beings, we are all committed to value them. Otherwise, it would be a contradiction in our commitment to value our own rational nature. In this way, Kant set up the foundation for our interest (to maintain the status of a rational being) to care for others and consider them as entities with rights. The question we must ask now is whether animals pertain to this standard of rights: Can animals be generalized as truly rational beings?

Opponents may argue that animals do in fact choose to do actions with intentional will, but they have failed to prove that such actions are either a product of intelligent instinct for survival or the repetitive training by others. In contrast, the intent of various actions by human beings has been proven to be rational when we, for example, display a logical analysis of ideas or when we make a continuous reflection on our past history to reach moral conclusions that judge certain actions as reprehensible and to participate in social movements to never repeat such incidents again. The fact that students from 40 countries are pouring out their logical and philosophical inquires in this event is also a sufficient example that hints at the faculties or qualities that differentiate human beings from animals. Thus, it can be said that the Kantian idea of rights, to a certain extent, proves that there is in fact a difference between human beings and animals and that, when there should be an inevitable prioritization between the two, the higher consideration must be for the former.

However, as a personal evaluation of this issue, I hope to show that—although fundamentally there may be no convincing argument that animals are as important as human beings—there is a way in which we can effectively promote considerable care for animals as well. The case for this stems from the agreement that the will of human beings is not only comprised of rationality—that is, although the identity of human beings is made as unique due to our rational nature, there are other qualities within us that could become the groundwork for why we should care for animals. Concluding that "animals have no rights equivalent to those of human beings because that's logical" is assuming that people are sociopaths who have no emotions and can only be successfully persuaded by a clear, logical explanation. In reality, this is not the case for the vast majority of people. Within every person there seems to be, along with the basic rational nature, the capacity to sympathize. This idea was elaborated upon by the famous modern philosopher, Richard Rorty.

Rorty claimed that human beings are more like entities that have the faculty to care for their own group, but sometimes fail to extend that love to other groups. Soldiers who valiantly protect their own country's women and children but inhumanely rape the women of the opposite nation or countries that are extremely assertive of the importance of human rights but neglect the genocides in other nations show this kind of nature. Thus, it is extremely effective to promote care and sympathy by showing the possibility for different groups to be actually connected together. For example, when the soldiers ask why they must care for the opponent country's women, we could suggest that those women are somebody else's wives and mothers, just like the soldiers' wives back home. Likewise, the progress of rights can actually be accelerated by not just an underlying complex foundation, but also the "progress of sympathy."

In that case, there is the possibility that we can—although we might not be able to identify them to be the same as us—connect animals with human beings and trigger such progress of sympathy. Animal rights activists show photos of the teardrops in the eyes of cows dragged to the slaughter house or condemn those who eat dogs by asking whether they would do the same thing to their domestic pets in order to show how human beings can readily relate to animals in a certain sense. Thus, I would like to propose that we should consider our complex nature that contains not just rationality, but also the capacity for sympathy and exploit that nature to create a heightened importance for the appropriate treatment of animals.

Furthermore, although it has been shown that human beings are distinctively different from animals and have the higher demand in rights, there could be more sophisticated analyses of whether the less significant rights of human beings can serve as a justification to neglect the extreme suffering of animals. That is, there could be a limit to particular human rights if they are not really necessary to uphold the rational identity of human beings and they happen to harm animals considerably and continuously. Thus, some people could righteously argue that the unlimited hunting of animals for mere entertainment should be restricted. Others could make a legitimate case that the abuses of animals within the food industry should be regulated.

Thus far, I have attempted to negate Singer's standard for rights— the existence of suffering and enjoyment—and focus more on whether there could actually be a fundamental justification for animal rights. After suggesting that there is in fact a notable distinct quality for human beings that fail to be extended to animals, I presented an alternative approach for addressing the present concern for the disrespect for animals. As an essay by a young student with limited experience and knowledge, this paper would probably have some fallacies and areas that require more in-depth analysis. However, I hope that it has contributed to the philosophical discussion of animal rights and touched upon some solutions for the realistic problems we face today. As a high school student who is immensely interested in the promotion of universal human rights, I believe this was a great opportunity for me to think about the other areas within the discussion of rights that might have been belittled in their importance.

PART II

KANT &
HUMAN RIGHTS

THE CATEGORICAL IMPERATIVE AND HUMAN RIGHTS

I looked down at *Groundwork of the Metaphysics of Morals* and took a deep breath. Digesting Immanuel Kant's words would obviously be a challenging task. I ambitiously opened up to the first page. In that historical magnum opus, Kant had established the categorical imperative, a key feature of his ethical system.

As the name suggests the categorical imperative is an absolute obligation that must stand in all conditions and situations. It is well-known in its formulation: "Act so that you use humanity in your person, as well as in the person of every other, always at the same time as end, never merely as a means."

The question that struck me was whether the categorical imperative is related to human rights. I was able to answer this inquiry through Professor Risse's course "Human Rights—A philosophical introduction." Professor Risse explained in his lectures how to derive the argument for the categorical imperative and how the concept is intertwined with the establishment of human rights.

The outline of the argument that derives the categorical imperative—"Act so that you use humanity in your person, as well as in the person of every other, always at the same time as end, never merely as a means"—starts with the premise that we are all "rational agents." As rational agents, we intentionally choose a certain course or goal of actions. By setting a goal or course of actions intentionally, we are essentially implying that something about the goal is valuable: It is worth pursuing. In other words, by doing an action, we are conferring or transmitting a value on an element of that action and deeming it as valuable. For example, if I choose to have pizza for lunch, it implies that the action of eating pizza for lunch beholds a certain merit or value.

According to the next step of the argument, in order to confer a value, an individual must be rationally committed to find value in him-/herself. Without being a "source" of values, an individual cannot pursue things and transmit value to them. Thus, as long as we acknowledge ourselves as rational agents, we have a commitment to value ourselves. The characteristic that defines us as rational agents— namely, intentionally choosing a certain course or goal of actions— requires us to become valuable and to value our rational nature.

The interesting point that Kant makes is that he subsequently extends the scope of discussion to include other people: Every other "rational being" would be in the same position as us. They would represent their existence in the same way. Thus, we must acknowledge that everybody else must value their rational natures for precisely the same reason as us. This ultimately means that, when an individual disregards and undermines another person and treats him/her "merely as a means," it would be equally degrading to his/her own capacity, which would be a contradiction of his/her own commitment to value him-/herself as a rational agent. Therefore, the categorical imperative holds that we must never use another person merely as a means, but instead value their rational natures as an end in itself—something that is unconditional and has independent worth.

Then how is the categorical imperative related to human rights? A right is essentially different from other general desires or needs. The following is an excerpt from an essay I wrote after going to Cambodia for volunteer work in 2011. It reveals a personal experience that helped me grasp the unique element of a right.

During my freshmen years, I went to Cambodia to teach children in impoverished towns. Fifty children were crammed in a deteriorating classroom. While I was teaching them English, rain suddenly started to pour down from the sky and water ferociously splashed into the room. When the children rushed to shut the wooden windows and door, the room—having no electricity—became pitch black. I awkwardly stood in the darkness and listened to the raindrops slamming down on the roof. Suddenly, another sound grasped my attention. From a corner of the darkness, a boy, unaffected by the circumstances, bashfully but confidently spoke.

"It's okay. Please teach."

It struck me then that there was something much more profound about the boy's timid but resolute request. It struck me that, amidst the blackness, he was asking for not just an English expression but a basic right to the education to which he was entitled. It felt like, amidst the blackness of negligence by the world, the children were demanding something we were obliged to give: fundamental rights.

The concept of rights is unique because it is not just a need or want. It is something that we can claim or demand. Immanuel Kant's categorical imperative is relevant to human rights because it touches upon this essential element that constitutes a right: the ability of an entity to make a legitimate demand of others for a course of action.

The categorical imperative answers a fundamental question: What would the nature of our relationship have to be for you to claim a moral right against me? That is, in order for a right to be grounded in principle, there must be an interest that is of significant importance to demand certain behavior from others. Kant's imperative explains that this interest would be the higher-order interest to become and remain as a person endowed with reason—namely, to remain a rational agent. If I disregard other peoples' rights and treat them merely as a means, I am failing to maintain that higher-order interest by falling into a contradiction: By degrading another rational agent, it would be equally degrading my own rational nature, something that I am committed to value.

So why is Kant's relevance to human rights significant? Personally, I believe that the Kantian system of ethics and the concept of human rights that it creates are significant in the sense that they offer an idea of universal rights without relying on theology, tradition, culture, or other external factors. By remaining independent from the external factors and being anchored toward the inner rational nature of each being, the Kantian system of ethics and human rights is a reasonably strong counter-case to the idea of the relativism of morality and rights.

Although controversy remains regarding whether the idea of universal human rights is beneficial or feasible in the first place, it is also undeniable that certain countries or individuals tend to justify their blatant human rights abuses too easily with relativism rhetoric, claiming that their unique characteristics somehow allow and even require such abuses. In contrary to this rhetoric, Kant urges that morality should be derived from the fundamental universal human nature. In that sense, his system of ethics can be acknowledged for contributing to the effort to find an acceptable, philosophical foundation for universal morality and universal human rights.

KANT'S DIGNITY AND HUMAN RIGHTS

"This house would legalize the sale of human organs."

W hile I was researching this very classical debate motion, I had the chance to really think about what human dignity means. The word *dignity* always seems to be tossed around in debates, in the classroom, in the media through politicians' speeches . . . but what did it really mean?

I decided to delve into more of Immanuel Kant and his concept of dignity. In Professor Risse's course, we could learn about not only what Kant thought dignity was, but also the intricate relationship it had with the notion of human rights.

To Kant, dignity refers to the worth of rational beings. In detail, Kant regarded rational beings as having three specific natures that made them have unconditional worth, or dignity:

1) Rational beings set goals and choose principles of action.
2) This choosing as an act of a rational being is subject to the categorical imperative.
3) Thus, rational beings are sources of all other values.

Likewise, Kant's definition of human dignity is directly connected with human agency and the ability to choose the course or principles of action. Thus, human dignity is not something that we necessarily have to strive to earn. It is very naturally bestowed to the rational nature of every rational being; as long as we remain in such a status, we cannot give this dignity or worth away. To explain this idea of dignity, we can look at two examples of legal decisions that embody Kant's idea of dignity. In fact, various legal systems reflect Kant's ideas, but the German constitutional law and legislation make particularly frequent significant references to the Kantian viewpoint of dignity.

The first example is Germany's legal decision that life imprisonment without parole is incompatible with the idea of human dignity and is thus illegal. Why would this be against the Kantian concept of human dignity? Kant's answer would have probably started off with the analysis that, although a wrongdoing might call for punishment and possibly for the forfeiting of certain rights, criminals still maintain their rational nature. As long as these criminals remain rational  agents, their basic dignity cannot be disregarded or stripped away. In other words, they cannot be deemed completely worthless. However, imprisoning people until death without parole implies the message that there is no chance or potential that these criminals will be worthy to society anymore. That is, there is no reason to even give these criminals the opportunity to be incorporated back into the society. This scenario is a fundamental breach and disregard of the idea of dignity because it deems the rational capacity of a criminal's life to be insignificant from a certain point.

The second example that reflects the Kantian notion of human dignity is Germany's legal decision that shooting down hijacked airliners when they are about to be used as weapons (like on September 11, 2001) is unconstitutional. Intuitively, the shooting down of a hijacked plane to prevent further harm seems quite reasonable. However, to Kant, the government's decision to shoot down hijacked planes would be essentially using the passengers on the plane as merely a means to protect the people on the ground. Using a group of rational beings as merely a means would be, as previously discussed, an act that disregards their rational nature. That is, the passengers deserve to have fundamental rights as rational beings, but the government would be failing to protect such rights if it shoots down people who are ironically the victims of an action and the most vulnerable citizens who are in dire need of protection.

Kant's notion of dignity is related to human rights in the sense that it requires—almost mandates—us to consider the implications that an action has on each and every individual. Thus, instead of placing each and every situation on a utilitarian weighing system, the concept of dignity forces us to look at the action through the lenses of the individuals being affected.

In more general terms, the notion of dignity simultaneously suggests that there is indeed a minimum standard that we are obliged to guarantee to every human being regardless of his/her race, gender, income, religion, language, or any other status. I remember how I watched a short Korean documentary made by EBS about human rights. The title of the documentary, *The Minimum List*, implied that there is indeed a point at which we must step in to say that there are certain, basic rights that we as human beings must honestly and humanely be granted.

This is probably why "The Universal Declaration of Human Rights" embodies the concept of dignity from the very first line of its Preamble:

> "Whereas recognition of the inherent dignity and of
> the equal and inalienable rights of all members of the
> human family is the foundation of freedom, justice,
> peace in the world,"

WHAT ABOUT UTILITARIANISM?

U tilitarianism is an ethical theory which states that the right course of action is that which "maximizes overall happiness" or "maximizes overall utility." The utilitarianist view is frequently contrasted with Kant's view: Utilitarianism is known to be a consequentialist thought stressing that the moral value of an action should be determined and judged by its resulting outcome. Kant's system of ethics is considered to be a deontological thought that judges the moral value of an action by its adherence to a rule or obligation and does not focus more on the results or consequences.

In this response paper, I will briefly present my ideas on the controversial subject of utilitarianism. As discussed in Professor Risses's class, the "greatest-happiness principle" has been criticized from a variety of angles. I reject the idea of basing our actions solely on the utilitarianist calculation for similar reasons. However, I also think that there are some specific and inevitable cases when the principle could be taken to consideration as a criterion for decision making.

In general terms, I think such situations would be when the state has to distribute its benefits/fulfill its duties but has limited resources and is really forced to choose. Of course, I agree that the overall rule for states should be to analyze each situation differently and think about the complex issues in every case. Unfortunately, there are inevitable and urgent situations when the state must make a choice. When the train is approaching and will inevitably kill either ten people on one track or one person on the other, the state will probably choose to save the greater number. Similarly, when the state must choose between helping two simultaneous humanitarian crises, it would save the side with more people in danger.

Although many people heavily criticize utilitarianism, when they become neutral actors in pressing and imminent circumstances, the majority will probably choose to save the greater number of people over the one person. I think it is natural to instinctively judge that if one person's life is so valuable, many more peoples' lives will be much more valuable; it is natural that, while watching the news and hearing about tragedies around the world, an individual feels more misery and sympathy when the number of injuries or deaths is greater. Likewise, I think the state is bound to think about the greatest-happiness principle when it is literally forced into such situations.

However, that does not mean that the state should endorse the utilitarianist calculation as its general rule for conduct and suddenly intrude upon the minority's basic rights or actively sacrifice them for the majority. The problem with utilitarianism is that it does not fully consider the impact of cracking down upon the minority for the majority. Although upholding the majority may seem to bring about greater utility, in reality we see that that is not always the case. Especially in today's world, people become enraged when governments try to justify their actions of persecuting the marginal for the so-called great cause. For example, when the public learned of the atrocities occurring at Guantanamo Bay, it was offended and upset, despite the government's claims that the prison camp was used to uphold national security.

Although utilitarianism did not really care for fundamental human rights and brushed the issue off as a trivial matter, actually even by its standard, infringing upon human rights is an act that brings dissatisfaction and less utility for the many because everyone is a minority in some sort of way or another. When the state blindly operates under the rule of the greater good, people are threatened about what will happen in other circumstances when they become the minority. In other words, utilitarianism does not really take into account the utility that comes from the comfort that we live under a government that actually cares for the most fundamental civil, political, economic, and social rights. Utilitarianism does not really take into account the utility people get from reassuring themselves that they live in a society that values human rights and advocates for the progression of such rights.

Contrary to utilitarianist views, in reality we do receive utility from ensuring human rights, which is probably one of the reasons why we have so many declarations, treaties, protocols, and conventions in order to ensure them. We do receive happiness from upholding the minorities' voices as well, which is why we see so many human rights activists and organizations that fight for them.

In conclusion, I think that utilitarianism—although it might be food for thought or even a criterion for deciding in inevitable situations—should not be the ultimate aim or guiding principle for both the state and individuals because the principle itself is insufficient as it does not consider one of the key elements of "utility."

A Philosophical Musing into Kantian Ethics

Immanuel Kant argued for an ethical system that finds morality from within. Since then, he has been recognized as one of the most influential moral philosophers. The following essay is an attempt to delve more deeply into the broad philosophical idea of Kantian ethics.

> "There are two things that fill the mind with ever new and increasing admiration and awe . . . the starry sky above me and the moral law within me."
>
> Immanuel Kant,
> *Critique of Practical Reason, Conclusion*

The world in which we live today includes an unprecedented prevalence of human rights talk and rhetoric, but the fundamental principle that proves the existence of inherent, natural rights tends to be absent or insufficient. The question has troubled philosophers for centuries: Do human beings indeed have the dignity and sanctity that grants them intrinsic rights? Furthermore, is there a universal morality that could be imposed on us all in order to protect such rights? In such a case, what will the moral system look like and where will it get its roots from?

Immanuel Kant, undoubtedly one of the greatest thinkers in human history, took a unique stance on the issue in his magnum opus *Critique of Practical Reason* and argued that we, as entities of reason, have moral laws within ourselves and thus can form a morality that extends to other people as well. In this essay, I will first delve into Kant's given quotation and analyze its meaning in context. I will then proceed to pose a few questions that need to be addressed more by Kant and discuss the limitations of a Kantian viewpoint on morality. The final parts of this essay will be spent examining further implications and my personal opinion on this issue.

Kant did not hesitate to make an early divergence from the mainstream thought of the day. He claimed that reason easily goes astray when we adamantly think that truth and knowledge can be found somewhere "out there." Instead of striving to understand the structures of the outside world, we should be tremendously interested about the structures that are formed by our own mind and reason. From that, Kant concluded that, if there is a system of morality, it cannot be found from external sources like God or religion (as many other philosophers claim), but from within ourselves and from the reason that dictates us.

An important premise of the Kantian view of morality is the idea that human beings are rational agents; we see inclinations as possible grounds for action and carefully decide whether to adopt such inclinations as principles or maxims. In an easier sense, rational agents do not base their actions merely on an irrational or instinctive heat-of-the-moment decision, but instead have the faculty to adopt certain rules for themselves and find patterns of regularity in their actions. The consecutive question that is asked and answered by Kant is whether there are restraints to the process of forming the rules and regularities. He declares that, if there really were restraints, they would be in the form of imperatives—either a hypothetical imperative or the renowned categorical imperative. The categorical imperative, according to Kant, was a rule that must be adhered to unconditionally simply because we are rational beings.

After constructing such layers of analysis, Kant finally reached the conclusion that, if there were a system of morality, it would 1) come from within rational beings and 2) be in the form of a categorical imperative. Kant's given quotation that "there are two things that fill the mind with ever new and increasing admiration and awe . . .—the starry sky above me and the moral law within me" is a demonstration of the unwavering strong belief that Kant has toward this conviction.

Although Kant was clearly successful in suggesting a fresh analysis of the source and form of morality, it seems that there are questions remaining to ask and answer. The paramount inquiry would be what Kant means about the concept of morality: What is truly moral? Before trying to answer this question and define the parameters of morality we could also doubt the implied premise that we can actually agree upon what morality is in the first place.

To view the concern in more general terms, morality is a guideline and rule of conduct based on what we deem to be right. As there is no fixed definition of what is right, the discussion of morality inevitably and necessarily opens up room for a value judgment. However, the problem arises because what we regard to be right depends on countless factors and ultimately differs for each individual. This is precisely why the utilitarianist, for example, holds a starkly different standard of morality, and Kant would never agree to his or her judging criteria of calculating utility. Likewise, it is virtually impossible to detect a moral law that is universally agreed upon by every individual.

Some may argue that this objection is unfair; they could say that in fact Kant did not aim to find a common ground amongst people but instead wanted to find an absolute set of rules that can be forced and demanded by others, regardless of personal differences. However, even in that case, one may ask for Kant's justification of the morality he assigned as the universal code of conduct and tried to impose. Again, from where does such morality come and why should people, who are idiosyncratically different, adopt a single set of laws somewhat arbitrarily chosen by others? Kant does not provide sufficient analysis about why his set of morality and rules can be the ultimate answer to what is right.

However, putting the justification issues aside, for more meaningful philosophical musing, I would like to move on to directly examine Kant's standard of morality and its validity. Kant's idea of morality is normally summarized into two sentences: 1) "Act only on that maxim whereby you can at the same time will that it should be a universal law" and 2) "act so as to treat people as ends in themselves, never as mere means." Although the two maxims can act as generally agreeable guidelines for conduct, it is doubtful whether they can be deemed as absolute and unconditional, as Kant claims. In that case, the maxims can no longer function as categorical imperatives, and Kant's view on morality loses much of the credibility it stands upon.

In order to examine the sensitive issues of this case, we could look at a real-life example. During the Holocaust, what was a homeowner to do if he were secretly hiding a Jewish family and the police come along to ask if there were any Jewish people in the house? Following Kant's line of morality, the homeowner would have to tell the truth, even though he knows that the Jewish family will be immediately killed or taken away after his words, because Kant stressed that it is pivotal to value the one-on-one relationships with others and—regardless of what is good for the general society or in the long run—follow our imperatives, one of which is not deceiving others. He further maintains that deceiving someone is using him or her as a means and not as an ends, which goes against the second standard of morality. However, reflecting back on the Jewish family example, we could ask the question of whether telling the truth was genuinely the right thing to do in the situation. The police officer is not based or grounded upon morally sound principles and the action of telling the truth will end innocent peoples' lives. In that case, it seems intuitively and rationally more morally right for the homeowner to weigh between his options and choose to protect the Jewish family.

In essence, the problem of Kant's categorical imperative when it comes to its practice is that it does not allow for the faculty that he himself most values: the faculty of reason. When Kant praises the power of rational thinking and reason but consecutively confines people under a rigid moral code, he is essentially limiting the scope by which people can rationally judge the countless shades of situations they will confront in real life. Especially in the situations in which two imperatives and two values clash, the agent is forced to make up his or her mind in the difficult dilemma. It is reason that enables people to decide what is morally permissible in dilemmas or exceptional cases, and such flexibilities should be incorporated into the imperatives that Kant presents. The justification for incorporating flexibility is actually proved through Kant's very own words that we are entities capable of judging rationally and employing reason.

The second question that I would ask to Kant relates to his description of the moral law. As can be inferred from the given quotation, Kant firmly believed that his moral code could serve as a law for the actions of people. The fact that something serves as a law implies that it transcends simple importance and amounts to the extent of being significant enough that we can mandate others to do certain actions. In other words, expanding the discussion to a moral law is necessarily extending the issue to rights. When everyone has a right, it also means that others have an obligation to protect such a right and is thus mandated to do so. Kant analyzed that we do have certain intrinsic rights that others are forced to protect due to the consistency of our commitments. In other words, an individual is committed to value his or her capacity to reason. However, as that is a capacity that exists in every other person as well, it would be a contradiction if we did not value others and infringe upon them. In a sense, every individual's value is rooted from the same source—reason—and, thus, we have the obligation to remain consistent in our commitments and uphold the rights of others as well.

Yet one question that could be posed here is whether the willingness of each individual to remain consistent is strong enough to override the countless incentives to be self-centered. Do individuals place that much value on trying to maintain consistent in thoughts and actions in the first place? Actually, many would agree that in fact inconsistency and bias are quite natural and prevalent elements of everyday life; as such, people will not be motivated to respect the rights of others due to the fear or hatred of becoming contradictory. Just because human nature has an inclination toward reason does not mean that people cannot make contradictions.

It is quite possible to make an argument that being inconsistent is actually a part of human nature; it is not so persuasive to force individuals to go against their nature to protect the dignity of others. In this sense, it can be said that Kant's universal moral law has a relatively low possibility to be grounded and practiced in reality. Even if we assume that it has no other fallacies and can function as a principle and theoretical proof for human rights, it cannot really fulfill its spirit of acting as a moral law if it is based upon unpractical premises.

The last question I would ask Kant is about the most defining characteristic of his moral philosophy: the analysis that he found the source of morality from within us—namely, from reason. Several unique concerns arise when we rely on a morality that is fundamentally dependent on rational thinking. In fact, reason can be very subjective and varied. For the same conclusions, there could be multiple different explanations that are logical and reasonable.

Even by employing pure reason we can reach different conclusions and answers to a single question. (This can be easily demonstrated in how great thinkers of the past centuries have reached a spectrum of ideas while they all profess to have adhered to reason.) Thus, when we allow the faculty of reason to have exclusive power and then depend upon it, we can be confused by the bombarding of numerous contrasting views. In the worst case, reason can be utilized to go directly against Kant's model of morality when self-interest and self-centeredness are rationally proven to be beneficial to individuals.

To illustrate, the society as a whole can employ pure reason to reach an explanation that in fact lying to each other is necessary in various cases. In such a case, no matter how Kant tries to dismiss such claims by presenting his categorical imperatives, his persuasion will be inevitably undermined because he is being objected by the very element—reason—on which he based his principles.

Likewise, we can see that the unprecedented emphasis on morality and rights coming from within ourselves can be a cultivated and insightful analysis, but can simultaneously be abused and distorted by others quite easily.

Up to this point, I have made a few jabs at the principles of one of the greatest thinkers in human history. Although my refutations will contain several limitations and thus the overall ideas generated by Kant will remain unwavering, I believe that this essay could provide some food for thought on how to strengthen the Kantian view of morality. Ultimately, I have tried to show that Kant's categorical imperatives are difficult to reach if we do not have a set agreement on what morality is, if individuals maintain their natural disposition for inconsistency and self-interest, and of we rely merely on the power of reason. However despite these limitations, I personally would say that the Kantian approach to morality remains significant and meaningful, especially in the 21st century, for two reasons.

The first would be that Kant regards people with an underlying sense of equality. He finds the value of each and every human being not from their differences, but from their inevitable similarities: the human nature of possessing reason. It is pivotal to adopt such views in the ever-changing and increasingly interacting era of globalization nowadays. We tend to look more at differences; even the current human rights rhetoric focuses on the disparity between states and cultures. However, there must be a more philosophical foundation as to why we human beings are to be equally valued for a nature that we all possess of regardless of external and internal idiosyncrasies.

The second significance and meaningfulness of Kant's approach would be that he directly refutes and tackles the idea of the relativism of morality and human rights. When countries justify their human rights abuses with relativist language, saying that their unique culture and unique racial characteristics allow and even require such abuses, it is hard to refute such talk with strong principles. However, Kant urges us not to find morality from external factors like culture, history, or the state of development, but rather from the fundamentally universal human nature. In this sense, Kant is successful in providing acceptable philosophical grounds for universal morality and universal human rights.

IS TORTURE MORALLY JUSTIFIED?

According to the definition given by the Convention against Torture(CAT) of the United Nations, torture is "any act by which severe pain or suffering, whether physical or mental is intentionally inflicted on a person for such purposes as obtaining from him or a third person information or a confession, punishing him for an act he or a third person has committed, or intimidating or coercing him or a third person, or for any reason based discrimination of any kind, of or with the consent or acquiescence of a public official or other person acting in an official capacity."

Immanuel Kant disagreed with the principle and practice of torture. To him, it was an action that completely or at least partially disregarded the rational capacity of an individual by deeming it as insignificant. The following essay delves in to this area of applied Kantian ethics. More specifically, it is a philosophical evaluation of Henry Shue's well-known article "Torture," which argued against the practice of torture in any situation.

The immorality of torture is too easily taken for granted. However the world today demands a much more sophisticated discussion. Global terrorism is no longer a theoretical discussion, but a reality; accordingly, torture is frequently suggested as an inevitable option that must be taken into consideration. This shift in global context mandates those who renounce torture to come up with not just an emotional appeal, but also both practical and principle foundations for their objections.

Henry Shue's article "Torture" is also an attempt to address the complexities of torture and ultimately argue for a case against its practice. This essay will explain and evaluate Shue's argument. In doing so, it will be in line with his general repudiation of torture while simultaneously pointing out several limitations of his viewpoint and suggesting alternative ways of analysis.

Shue principally rejects torture because he says it exploits the defenseless. In other words, victims of torture are essentially void of a way to escape the attack. To explain this idea, Shue presents two major types of torture: terroristic torture and interrogative torture. In the former type, victims have no say over the extent of their pain because the goal of terroristic torture is to plant terror in the minds of potential opponents of the state. Thus, there is no way the victim can elude the affliction through compliance as the amount of torture is not proportionate to his or her response, but rather the impact it has to a third party.

However. even in the case of purely interrogative torture, which is restricted to the minimum necessary standard—which, according to Shue, happens extremely rarely in view of the "strength and nature of a torturer's likely passions"—the defenseless is fully and inevitably exploited. To address interrogative torture, Shue categorizes possible victims of torture into groups—the innocent bystander, the ready collaborator, and the dedicated enemy—and claims that in all three cases, "the apparent possibility of escape through compliance tends to melt away upon examination."

According to him, the guiltless bystander might not be able to decisively prove his or her innocence and inability to comply. The ready collaborator will not be able to comply and make a bargain because of the torturer's doubt about when the maximum compliance has happened. The devoted opponent will not be able to make a concession as collaboration would be a betrayal and denial of his or her highest values, which would not constitute a genuine escape. An escape, Shue argues, must be an alternative that is not only "preferable but also itself satisfies some minimum standard of moral acceptability."

Although Shue provides insights on practical aspects and tendencies of torture, his analysis is based on several premises that have yet to be established. The first assumption he makes is that the state (here, the torturer, according to CAT's definition of torture: "with the consent or acquiescence of a public official or other person acting in an official capacity") has no particular reason to reduce the suffering of victims in instances of terroristic torture. This assertion might be true if the torturers live in a vacuum that includes only the victims and potential enemies.

However, in reality, the impact of another immensely significant third party—namely, the general public—must be taken into consideration. The government and public officials, for both practical and principle reasons, have strong incentives to listen to the voices of their domestic constituents or the international community. When the general public firmly disapproves of an action and expresses such condemnation, the government is heavily pressured to put an end to it. Thus, as long as there are people who oppose the use of torture, the government does have a clear reason to be careful not to step over a certain extent of brutality in terroristic torture situations.

To illustrate, when people were enraged over the alleged torture and abuse at Guantanamo Bay, the government was swift to notice: President Obama renounced the prison and promised to close it. A World Public Opinion.org poll conducted in 2008 found that, of 19 nations, in 14 of them most people favor an unequivocal rule against torture. Once we consider such popular disapproval toward brutality and the public's increased power to scrutinize the government and make it accountable, Shue's analysis on terroristic torture is largely undercut.

Another unsubstantiated assumption by Shue is that a victim being virtually defenseless is a situation unique to torture. At the onset of his argumentation, Shue claims that fighting in war (while abiding the laws of war) at least provides the opportunity for a fair fight by protecting those who are completely defenseless, such as noncombatants and POWs.

On the other hand, he continues, torture involves an unconstrained actor inflicting pain on those who are utterly stripped of any means to defend themselves. With this distinction, Shue formulates the reason why torture is uniquely more abhorrent than other forms of violence, such as killing during combat. However this difference seems arbitrary. The vast majority of wars involve a dominant side and a weaker side, and when the gap between the two forces is wide, the combat itself cannot stand as a fair fight. If a group of weaponless combatants is surrounded by a mass of opponents armed with the best equipment available (not a rare situation at all), any rational observer would conclude that the combatants actually do not have a fair chance to defend themselves. Thus, one could ask the question: With what standards does Shue judge a victim to be defenseless and would those features be truly exclusive to torture? It seems precarious for Shue to base his major principle for illegitimating torture on a vague distinction that has not been fully corroborated.

The third premise that requires further elaboration is that "uncertainty about when the fullest possible compliance has occurred" puts the innocent bystander and the ready collaborator in a state of constant threat from torture. Although Shue's reasoning demonstrates the possibility of such risk, it is insufficient to make a generalization. Moreover, it is an exaggeration to say that such risk is significant enough to make the bystanders and collaborators defenseless. To begin with, the issue of uncertainty is not as significant as Shue portrays it to be. We are not always blinded by ignorance of who knows how much information; there are numerous mechanisms employed to investigate and discern who is innocent and who is guilty and to what degree. To say that no one can ever decisively demonstrate his or her innocence or irrelevancy with a certain crime is essentially undermining the reason for the existence of a criminal justice system.

Furthermore, if a torturer really did continue to interrogate and harass an innocent bystander, it is unfair to point to this as an inherent flaw of torture; this is an apparent abuse of the practice, in which the torturer is ignoring the fundamental established rule of presumed innocence. Therefore, although Shue's points offer the tendency of how torture is carried in a notorious manner, they fall short of qualifying as a principle ground for objection.

The last question one may justifiably pose relates to Shue's claim that a committed adversary is not granted a preferable and morally acceptable route to elude torture. The major problem of this discourse comes from its ambiguity. What constitutes a preferable alternative is ultimately a subjective matter and can differ for every individual. What counts as morally admissible is also a controversial subject that has not been completely agreed upon. Another problem that must be attended to is the fact that Shue never gives a reason as to why an escape must be provided for individuals who are essentially devoted to harm the state. He may be taking for granted that even criminals have basic human rights, but then again there is no rationale for why the opportunity to escape is an inherent right. Especially when the individual is an obvious enemy of the state, why should the government place the criminal's preferences over the security of its citizens, whom it is obliged to protect? As a comparison, serial killers who are sentenced to death are not given a more desirable and moral option to avoid their punishment. Why should terrorists be bestowed with such grace?

An observation of Shue's argument seems to demonstrate that he is opposed to the usage of torture in any instance and with any type of victim. However, after developing his case, Shue reluctantly admits an exception to it: the ticking time bomb case. He "can see no way to deny the permissibility of torture in a case *just like this*" because of 1) the magnitude and certainty of the harm involved, 2) the greater supervision, and 3) the rarity of occurrence. The complication of these three justifications is that they are vague, applicable to any other situation, or factually incorrect. To make his point effective, Shue should offer criteria by which to determine harms are excused due to their significance and imminence. Otherwise, many cases of torture can be twisted to fit the ambiguous standard and be explained as time-ticking, momentous situations.

The second issue of careful supervision and medical assistance is deficient as it is not a concrete foundation for belief, but rather a technical matter that can be artificially controlled. Having more doctors or governmental officials to oversee the torturing scene is a condition that can be applied to any other case, and thus is inadequate as a justification to make the ticking time bomb case a unique exception. The last analysis point of how rare such incidents occur is increasingly proven to be false. Shue's article (which is more than 30 years old) clearly does not account for the changing global context—9/11, bombings in Mumbai, Morocco, Istanbul, Madrid, and the unprecedented war on terror. With the rise of terrorism, ticking time bomb situations are simultaneously increasing; today, these occurrences cannot be simply dismissed or considered as abnormalities.

Instead of relying on contingent justifications, torture could be permissible in ticking time bomb cases for a different rationale: These cases should be distinguished from other general interrogative torture instances because, in a ticking time bomb scenario, the victim has the higher hold in the balance of power. By remaining silent, he or she can inflict much more harm on the state than the state can possibly inflict on the victim through torture. Thus, the entire state is essentially fighting against something to which only the victim has a solution. In such a situation, the victim cannot be characterized as defenseless; rather, he or she holds the ultimate decision power. Thus, in the ticking time bomb scenario, we should consider the state to be in a continual process of war and active combat.

In an ideal world, torture should never be permitted. It is a morally troubling act that undermines the victims' most fundamental rights. Therefore, in general instances, it can never be considered a viable option as the utter deprivation of another's rights is too big a sacrifice to make for the fear of a possible threat. However, the world is not an ideal place, and exceptions exist that must be addressed. The ticking time bomb scenario is an actuality that we must confront, and only in such situations should torture be used as a last resort because the state is in fact engaged in a dangerous combat.

PART III
INTERNATIONAL POLITICS & HUMAN RIGHTS

"Universal" Human Rights? The Western View vs. the Eastern View

Human Rights

It is hard to say that we have reached a concrete, one-and-only definition of what human rights are. However, the general consensus is that human rights are fundamental rights to which we are entitled simply because we are human beings. This definition itself seems to imply one of the most important qualities of human rights: universality. That is, we have human rights simply because we are born with the status of a human being, not because we have a certain ethnicity, gender, wealth, political stance, or any other additional external factor.

Our aspiration held for the universality of human rights can be seen most clearly through the Universal Declaration of Human Rights, a historical declaration deemed to be "something profoundly new" because it was one of the biggest efforts to institutionalize the idea of rights in collaboration with universal values. The following is from its well-known preamble, which sets the tone and reflects the purpose of the declaration:

"Therefore THE GENERAL ASSEMBLY proclaims THIS UNIVERSAL DECLARATION OF HUMAN RIGHTS as a common standard of achievement for all peoples and all nations, to the end that every individual and every organ of society, keeping this Declaration constantly in mind, shall strive . . . ."

Writing the specifics of the declaration took a considerable amount of time; it had to be designed to be broadly representative of the global community and to incorporate the frequently conflicting views of different countries. The spectrum of the representative nations included Australia, Belgium, Chile, China (considered the "voice of east Asia"), Egypt, France, India, Iran, Lebanon (considered the "voice of Middle East"), the Philippines, the Union of Soviet Socialist Republics, the United Kingdom, the United States of America, and more.

However, contrary to the ideals reflected by the Universal Declaration of Human Rights, some issues hint that the idea of a universal standard for human rights is difficult to achieve. The example discussed earlier of Germany's decision to outlaw shooting down hijacked planes could serve to show that the views on concepts such as rights, dignity, or morality can be quite different. Similarly, the controversial debate concerning women wearing the burka (burqa) or other face veils shows that each side has compelling arguments. So could the standard, priority, or extent of what constitutes a human right differ according to country, religion, culture, or another factor?

If we take a step back and look more closely at the history of the Universal Declaration of Human Rights, it is hard to say that we have actually reached a consensus through the declaration. Saudi Arabia called the declaration a "violation of Islamic Law" and Iran criticized it as "a secular understanding of the Judeo-Christian tradition." In fact, after the declaration was created and ratified, additional declarations such as the "Cairo Declaration of human rights in Islam" or the "Bangkok Declaration" followed, arguing for "Muslim values" and "Asian values." Regardless of religious or cultural values, some people have differing views on even the specifics of the declaration—some argued that the idea of compulsory education was a violation of the right to peacefully follow one's own wills.

The conclusion? The gap between our ideals and reality is quite large. However, I believe such disparity is never a reason to either give up our ideals or adamantly push forward with them (as many countries currently do). In fact, I think it is chiefly important to develop a deeper understanding of why these differences exist. It is meaningful to refrain from looking at issues through exclusively our own lens. We must make the effort to understand the root cause of the disparity and then take steps to create an equilibrium or balance.

Back in the mid 1990s, the controversial "Asian values" debate emerged. Several Asian leaders, most representatively former Prime Minister Lee Kuan Yew from Singapore, argued that Asia had a unique set of values and ideologies primarily due to historical and cultural reasons. This essay will shed more light on this specific issue of how the concept of human rights is viewed differently in the Eastern perspective and Western perspective.

The most significant distinction comes from the fact that the principle subject of rights is different. By and large, the Western view of human rights (and rights in general) is that the subject of such rights is the individual. Various Western philosophical thoughts put forth by great thinkers such as Descartes, Rousseau, Rawls, and Kant reflect such focus on the individual. Indeed, ideas such as free will, *Cogito ergo sum* ("I think, therefore I am"), or the sacredness of dignity demonstrate the unique focus on each individual. In essence, human rights are thought of as the right to claim the qualities that allow every individual to live humanely as an absolute individual.

Contrary to this, the Eastern view of human rights starts off with the subject of the rights being society. The government should focus on maximizing the rights of the entire society. Confucianism, which truly and greatly influenced the Eastern thought system, does not contain or promote the concepts of an absolute individual. In fact, the starting point of Confucian values is the fact that we have certain relationships with other people. The Chinese character for person (人間) is a combination of the character that stands for human being and the character that stands for between, implying a person can achieve the sense of existence through the relationships he or she makes between himself/herself and another being. Similarly, the core ideology of Confucianism, benevolence (仁), is a notion that implies the importance of not just each individual, but the broader society that many individuals make together. (The Chinese character for benevolence is formed using the characters that stand for human being and two)

An example that shows this idea of a more community-based concept of rights could be China's controversial one-child policy. Regardless of the alleged societal benefits, it is predictable that many Western countries would strongly dissent to the implementation of the policy for the principle reasons that it undermines dignity or the basic right to pursue happiness.

The next distinction between the Eastern and Western views of human rights is the different priorities they have for differing types of rights. In general, the Western perspective emphasizes civil and political rights. The concepts of freedom and liberty against the oppression of a greater power have always been one of the core principles behind the Western idea of human rights. In the Western view, the government should be more "of the people, by the people," and the concept of social contract implies that, although the government is necessary, it should simultaneously be put under an active check-and-balance system by the people.

However, the Eastern perspective tends to place more emphasis on economic, social, or cultural rights. The greater focus is on politics "for the people" or leaders who rule with grace and boon. This thought can be better understood when we observe that many Eastern philosophers, including Confucius, stressed the importance of social roles and the adherence to such roles. Thus, it was important for a king to act like a king, a father like a father, a servant like a servant, and a son like a son. The king's role was to provide the economic, social, and cultural rights to his people, and the general public had its own specific role within the society. Although concepts such as Mencius's "dynastic revolution" or "dynamic cycles" emerged, such revolutions did not necessarily touch upon the concept of civil and political rights (such as the American or French revolution), but rather dealt with situations such as population decrease, famine, poor distribution of wealth, or civil war.

This winter vacation, I was given the opportunity to work as an intern at SUARAM, an active human rights NGO in Malaysia. SUARAM specializes in protecting and promoting civil and political rights. During the week I spent inside their small but passionate office, I had several discussions with the executive director and other workers. The discussion that struck me most was that, in Malaysia, civil and political rights are the lower priority; even from the local Malaysian people, civil and political right NGOs receive less support and resources compared to those working for economic and cultural rights. The executive director of SUARAM told me how she envied South Korea for its fast and relatively stable establishment of democracy more than its economic prosperity.

With this thought in mind, if we take another closer look at the Universal Declaration of Human Rights, it could be understandable why some Eastern countries might have accused the document of being centered more upon Western values. The preamble, which sets the tone and purpose of the rest of the declaration, specifically contains phrases such as:

> ". . . a world in which human beings shall enjoy freedom of speech and belief . . ."
> ". . . as a last resort, to rebellion against tyranny and oppression . . ."

However, I personally believe that this is never a justification for stopping the search for a universal standard for human rights. In fact, after we develop a deep understanding about why certain differences occur in viewpoints, it is important to take a step further. Instead of simply continuing to search for what is different, we should make efforts to reveal the blatant human right abuses that are simply morally wrong. Cases such as sexually abusing minors,  acid terror toward women, or genocide show that there can be and must be some standard of what is grievously and undeniably wrong according to any standard.

If we cannot immediately find a set, holistic universal standard for human rights, we should build specific ways to prevent and eliminate such cases that are blatantly wrong. To be fair, the United Nations is currently striving to do so, with its major conventions that have legally binding power (e.g., United Nations Convention Against Torture, Convention on the Rights of Child, Convention on the Elimination of All Forms of Discrimination against Women, Convention on the Right of Persons with Disabilities). The ratification and actual practice of these specific conventions should be pushed forward more vigorously, and more resources should be channeled toward specifically tackling the disparity issues amongst various cultures, religions, etc.

The concept and standard of human rights are not crystal clear or completely agreed upon. There are deeply rooted differences according to various factors that will be hard to compromise. However, these are not reasons to be discouraged. Rather, they should serve as the strong motivation that it is our important job to make a clearer, more comprehensive notion of human rights by promoting further discussion and debate.

INTERVENTION
IN THE NAME OF HUMAN
RIGHTS?

C hen Guangcheng's escape story is not just an exciting personal recount. The story of the Chinese civil rights activist—the "barefoot lawyer"—fleeing from house arrest into the U.S. Embassy in Beijing received immense international attention. The fact that the U.S. State Department, the British Foreign Secretary, Human Rights Watch, and Amnesty International appealed for this Chinese man's freedom was indeed a symbolic event that highlighted the effect of another country intervening into a sovereign nation's domestic policies in the name of human rights.

In practice, there are various substantial and realistic concerns related to the issue of international intervention. The obvious problem would be that controversies could arise according to which actors are involved in the intervention. For example, when the United States of America tries to intervene in China, the humanitarian action could be interpreted as a political or economic one. We also cannot exclude the possibility that the intervening nation has another external motivation, as many previous cases of intervention have repeatedly shown to be true. Another problem would be the possible backlash toward the intervention on the grounds of the action being a violation of national sovereignty. However, in this short essay, I would like to take a step back from the specifics to focus more on the principle matters of the debate and what it really boils down to.

International intervention is not a concept that immediately developed as soon as we had a global community. In fact, the concept of national sovereignty had much more weight and support than the notion of countries meddling with each others' affairs. Reading articles about the Syrian civil war, I intuitively felt the need to do something to help the tens of thousands of innocent citizens who have been mercilessly sacrificed. However, as I flipped through the newspaper some more and reached the editorials, I found myself reading through the many reasons why involvement and intervention are not the answer.

Most strikingly, the more editorials and opinions I read, the more I came to realize that, in fact, a considerable number of people believe that we have no moral justification or obligation to intervene in the first place. To think about the issue in easier terms, I started to ponder another situation: When I am a passerby and I see a man drowning in the river, do I have the moral obligation to save him? At first, I could not really find a concrete, philosophical reason for why we have a moral obligation to help that drowning man.

Yet thinking about the issue in deeper terms, I started to find more, not fewer, reasons for why we must save the drowning man (or the other nation that needed help). We might hesitate and not even want to save the man if he were a complete stranger. However, I am pretty sure that the majority of people would save a drowning person who is related—at least in some way—to themselves. I am also quite positive that there is a moral obligation for us to save another person when there is the possibility that we might have caused his or her plight. I reckoned the difference between the first situation and the latter two situations was the element of connection—that is, we have a stronger moral urge to save a person we know well or a person we have caused to be in trouble because we understand that we are somehow connected to that person. In the past, we might have felt less connected to the people and situations that are beyond our own borderlines. However, in this new era, we are undoubtedly becoming more interconnected every moment. The concept of a global village is not just a good sound bite; it is the new reality.

I believe it is naïve to assume that just because an event happens a few more miles away it is entirely detached from us. I believe it is plausible to say that every issue can be connected—that the poverty in another nation did not just happen because of the fault of that country independently. In that case, I  believe that it is simply natural and morally right that concepts such as the responsibility to protect (or R2P as many people call it now) have emerged from the ashes of the notion of an absolute national sovereignty. The idea that national sovereignty is a sacred, supreme and uncontrollable permission for reckless acts seems to be obsolete in this era.

To further discuss my personal viewpoint specifically on the issue of whether we can intervene in another nation's policies in the name of human rights, I think intervening is principally justified because human rights should be one of our highest priorities. When a certain nation is significantly threatening its citizens' most basic human rights, such as the right to life or the security of the person, I believe it could be argued that others have not only the justification, but also the duty to take action to defend such human rights. Perhaps it could also be argued that international intervention is an extension of the social contract theory. According to this theory, governments can and may use coercive actions or force to protect human rights. The reason why we have death penalties or physical punishments is because certain criminals violate basic human rights, and the government should impose threats of force to prevent and stop them. Thus, every individual in a society is given their free agency and absolute sovereignty over themselves when they respect the basic human rights of others. By the same logic—as sovereign nations are really nothing more than a group of individuals—if sovereign nations invade individuals' human rights, then other governments ought to be able to engage in even physical ways.

Finally, neglecting crimes such as genocide or prolonged civil wars in other nations just because they are foreign affairs implies that the people in one country have human rights worth defending while people in another country do not have the same rights worth protecting. This goes against the premise we have of fundamental moral equality of human beings. When the government's duty is to protect its citizens and another country is blatantly abandoning such duty and taking a further step to commit crimes against humanity that carry a brutality beyond our imagination, we should not just stand by because we are limited by something as artificial as a national border.

A Victim Who "Agreed": Reflection on FGM

The sphere of human rights has rapidly expanded from a domestic and local level into a truly global scale. Concepts such as the responsibility to protect have emerged as the new paradigm in the age of globalization, in which international security has become a major concern. Following the repeated failures of the international community to put an end to crimes against humanity, there has been increased momentum for international intervention as a legitimate and necessary method to prevent such human rights abuses.

This essay sheds light on the philosophical debate of international intervention, focusing on the situation from a fresh angle. The premise of interventions is usually that the victims are in dire circumstances and need help. However what if—for a cultural, historical, or any other reason—the victims have agreed to the suffering?

Globalization has undoubtedly opened us up to new realms and cultures. Cultural relativism rests on the premise that each culture has its own way of living and we must not judge it by another culture's standard of morality. A major criticism to this theory is that those who justify human rights abuse with cultural relativism rhetoric are predominantly those in power; they cannot represent the views of the victims. In his paper "Human Rights as a Neutral Concern," Scanlon focuses on this intriguing issue. He extends the philosophical debate by asking two questions: (1) If the victims have agreed to suffering and abuse, can we judge their consent to be wrong? (2) Is the attempt to protect such victims an improper act of cultural superiority?

The immediate reaction to Scanlon's first inquiry is that it centers upon a seemingly improbable situation. It seems absurd that an entire community of people would gladly subject themselves to be victims and abandon their most basic human rights for no particular reason. However, if there were the unnatural case in which victims did comply with such circumstances, we must be skeptical of whether such compliance indicates genuine agreement. Active opposition to a deeply rooted cultural practice triggers immense social backlash; societies use powerful formal and informal tools such as shunning to induce passive conformity. Thus, in this specific scenario, it is erroneous to apply the logic of "silence is consent."

For example, we cannot conclude that North Korean people genuinely approve of their totalitarian government just because they remain reticent to speak against it. It should be noted that in fact the significant minority of North Korean people have recently protested against the government, demanding food and electricity. The ongoing wave of North Korean refugees is also evidence that not all people approve of their leaders.

To address the first issue more directly, we cannot prove an opinion to be wrong as it is not a factual statement, but ultimately a decision made upon one's values. *De gustibus, non disputandum*: There is no disputing matters of taste. However it can be argued that the victims were forced into making a false choice without being sufficiently informed. To make this case, we must analyze the distinct nature of culture. The legitimacy of a culture does not necessarily come from rational reasoning. It gains authority through tradition and the legacy of predecessors who have gone through the same process.

Moreover when the culture is unique, it frequently becomes a source of in-group identity. Thus, individuals find themselves in a society in which a particular culture has already become the norm. Instead of a coherent explanation of why they must sacrifice certain rights, the victims learn about the isolation and discrimination they will confront when they opt out. They are simultaneously educated and systematically assured that every person before them experienced the same ritual and through that experience has become, allegedly, better off. If this is the case, can we say that the victims were given a proper opportunity to think about the issue rationally and judge independently?

Another scenario would be a society that is remote or deliberately detached from the rest of the world; consequently, the victims have no possible source of knowing about the alternatives. These circumstances make it easier for the individuals to be "brainwashed" and deluded that their culture is not unique, but rather universal and natural. This explains why highly controversial cultural practices often happen in relatively isolated places. In either scenario, although we cannot decisively declare the victim's consent to be wrong, we can safely conclude that the preponderance of such opinions is rooted in a false choice. When a person is in a situation in which it is extremely difficult to make a genuine decision, consent does not translate into concrete permission. This concept is well bound into our legal system. For example, we presume that children are not in the position to actually consent and, therefore, we criminalize adults who have sexual relationships with "willing" children. Likewise, when we consider their circumstances, it is naïve to assume that the victims' acceptance of suffering should grant legitimacy to and justification for the actions carried out against them.

To engage with Scanlon's second question, it is not just recommended but rather pivotal that we attempt to defend the victims. Whether such an attempt becomes an arrogant display of cultural superiority depends on the specific approach and manner taken. The other option—refraining from aiding victims because "they live like that"—can be thought of as negligence and just another form of superiority. It is equivalent to saying that we would not tolerate a situation for ourselves, but they can be allowed to suffer. Rather than completely ignoring blatant human rights abuse by assigning it to a different cultural context, we must attempt to act.

First, the vast majority of nations have—by signing and ratifying the Universal Declaration of Human Rights and/or the six core conventions (Convention on the Rights of the Child, International Covenant on Civil and Political Rights, International Covenant on Economic, Social and Cultural Rights, Convention on the Elimination of All Forms of Discrimination against Women, Convention on the Elimination of All Forms of Racial Discrimination, Convention against Torture and other Cruel, Inhuman or Degrading Treatment or Punishment)—already pledged their commitment to human rights.

This pledge can be seen explicitly in the Universal Declaration of Human Rights itself with the words "Whereas Member States have pledged themselves to achieve, in co-operation with the United Nations, the promotion of universal respect for and observance of human rights and fundamental freedoms." Not only have they made that general pledge, but ratifying member states are also directly accountable for human rights abuse they commit under the name of cultural relativism. For example, Egypt, one of the first countries to sign the Convention on the Rights of the Child, allows widespread genital mutilation of girls under the age of 18. This breaches multiple articles of the convention, such as the rights to health or privacy; thus, it is justifiable to pressure the Egyptian government to adhere to the rules to which they have legally committed themselves.

However, along with this legal obligation, people have the right to be involved in political activism to express their opposition toward certain cultures that commit horrendous actions that completely disregard even the bare minimum of rights. Such actions can become an offense against humanity as a whole. That is, the fact that such atrocities are condoned and even encouraged could be a threat that crosses borders. The phrase "crimes against humanity" is used to refer to precisely those "atrocities tolerated or condoned by a government or de facto authority" which "constitute a serious attack on human dignity." What is more, in this unique era of globalization in which countries are inevitably intertwined or even interdependent, the matters of other communities cannot be insignificant simply due to their physical distance; they approach us as much more intimate and compelling issues of universal concern. "No man is an island." No culture is an island.

The extent of the attempt to protect victims depends on the severity of the abuse, but the minimum threshold of any such endeavor should be suggesting the possibility of an alternative. A recommended example would be the Tostan Project, which aims to empower African communities through education and bring about positive social transformation.

This organization contributed immensely in the recent movements spreading in Senegal to end genital cutting. Likewise, when victims express their refusal to participate in the abusive practices, we must take further measures that pressure the authorities to put an end to them. A relevant example would be the multilateral economic sanctions imposed on the South African government to end apartheid. However, if the worst case scenario happens and the majority of the victims still accept the actions against them, asylum must be granted for the minority who choose to refuse and dissent.

The major refutation against the analysis thus far could be that the victims have a right to refuse to listen to the alternatives. In other words, they have a right to stay unmindful of other viewpoints and practice their culture in privacy; teaching them things they do not want to accept is a form of forcing and is thus a display of cultural imperialism. To respond, first we must question the premise that informing others of certain aspects is a display of cultural superiority.

When the Tostan Project taught local residents about the negative effects of genital mutilation and the right to bodily autonomy, was this really a situation in which foreigners came and proved or forced in any way that their culture was better? The concept of culture is a greatly complex matter that encompasses multiple different elements. An appreciation for basic rights or the knowledge of particular medical facts does not translate into a distinct culture. Likewise, even if a community eradicates one of its rituals after education, it does not necessarily mean their culture has been significantly undermined and altered. Cultures are not fixed concepts, but living entities that learn and change.

In addition, even if we assume that this attempt were an uncomfortable instance of cultural superiority, the harms must be weighed. Relativists tend to assume that cultural superiority is the worst possible harm, but is a pompous display of knowledge worse than having horrendous human rights abuses prolonged? Curiously, relativists are often absolutists when it comes to the inflexibility of their opinions: Why are their opinions about the superiority of certain cultures also not just opinions?

Finally, if the endeavor to help is somehow a coercive action, it should be noted that such risk of coercion is not unique; it has been a structural problem even when there was no interference at all. The community, through its deeply rooted traditions, has already virtually forced the victims to make a hardly independent decision to comply with the cultural norm. If the community that harms compels, why may not the community that rescues? Comparing this to the consequences of neglecting the problem entirely, society's implicit and explicit pressure still exists, but in addition to such coercive atmosphere, the endemic suffering and pain from the cultural norm continues. To be slightly more extreme, one could even argue that a forceful measure of protecting the victims might be necessary to counterbalance the immense pressure from which they currently suffer.

Under normal circumstances, safeguarding individuals from harms they voluntarily accept seems like an unnecessary overreaction. Yet when the context is a cultural one in which individuals are in uniquely difficult positions to choose for themselves, assistance from an outsider usually does more good than harm. No matter how valuable culture might be to a person's life, there must be a limit; if a culture actively and fully undermines the very life that it is supposed to enrich, it has crossed the line. In that case, it is both our moral obligation and right to assist victims to make a genuine decision and to pressure the community for change within the oppressive culture.

PART IV

HUMAN RIGHTS IN KOREA

BETWEEN UNBEARABLE
FURY AND LEVEL-HEADED
RATIONALITY

Recently in Korea, one of the major human rights concerns is the increasing rate of sex crimes, especially those targeted to children under 13. This essay was written to discuss some of my personal reflections upon the issue. It touches upon both the philosophical and practical aspects of sex crimes against children.

The Naju child rape incident.

A seven-year-old child who was sleeping peacefully in her bed was kidnapped and raped under a bridge. Reading the full account in the newspaper, my eyes were shaking and I choked at the indescribable pain the young girl must have experienced. The only thing society could give the girl was surgery to stitch up her burst rectum and an outcry of fury toward the criminal.

"We have to tear him into pieces!"

"That beast should be put into greater pain than death!"

Right now, Korea and I are shaking in unbelievable fury and hatred, but this sort of anger seems so . . . familiar. Indeed, Ms. Kong's book *Dogani (Silenced)* revealed the horrendous case of the ongoing, habitual sexual abuse of deaf children. Meanwhile, four years ago, an eight-year-old girl was dragged into a church bathroom, raped, and disabled for the rest of her life (the "Cho Do-Sun incident"). As sad as the reality is of ongoing sexual violence carried out against children in Korea, it is regretful that we as the public are also becoming exhausted of simply crying out in fury every time these incidents occur. Although I acknowledge that it is difficult to say we must "control our emotions" at this point, when the scars of the seven-year-old girl still have not faded, I will carefully argue that—in order to achieve genuine and effective justice—we cannot be enslaved by our own fury and emotions.

One year ago, Norway—the "land of peace"—was thrust into great shock and horror when a right-wing extremist and anti-Muslim terrorist took the lives of 77 people. Norway ultimately overcame its sadness not through more hatred and anger, but through more peace and more flowers of condolence. Norway's Prime Minister Jens Stoltenberg gave a moving speech, promising that Norway will not be a nation that the terrorist dreamt of: It will not become a nation full of exclusive hatred and division. Instead, the nation would fight back against the terrorist attack with more peace, more love for humanity, and more magnanimity. Likewise, I believe that, in order to completely eradicate a crime, we need to go in the complete opposite direction of the criminals and make society a hard place for criminals like them to live in.

The common characteristic of child sex offenders is that they have already lost their rationality. The reason why we frequently criticize them for having refused to be a human being or why we call them beasts is because they have failed to embody one of the major characteristics that define us as human beings: the ability to think reasonably and rationally. Thus, we need to go in the direct opposite direction of those who chose the utmost extreme and radical ways to fulfill their desires. We must be swift but reasonable, calm but tireless in seeking for justice and the right way to fight against such crimes.

The problem of being swayed by our emotions is that the necessary discussion for methods to prevent further crimes and to protect the current victims can be simply eclipsed by the overheated debate on how to make the criminal suffer in maximum pain. Actually, only a few days after the Naju child rape incident, another horrendous crime happened in which a pregnant women was raped inside her house. The sadder fact is that the victim could not receive adequate compensation from the government because she had no apparent external injuries. Another problem that can emerge if we get swayed by our emotions is that the public's demand for stronger penalties, such as castration or capital punishment, could be easily misconstrued as a temporary outburst of fury instead of being a legitimate public opinion.

What we must do after controlling our emotions is to seek for and establish principle, philosophical foundations for why sexual crimes against children are equally or even more serious wrongdoings compared to other felonies. That is, it seems inadequate to say that our reasons for reviving the death penalty—which has not been implemented in Korea for 15 years—under the claim that sexual crimes against children just feel horrendous and gruesome. There must be a sturdier foundation than our obscure feelings.

The reason why many countries regard torture as an especially serious crime and have even created a UN convention to stop the use of torture (United Nations Convention against Torture) is that torture makes the victim completely defenseless. I believe sex crimes against children are no different. By attacking children as young as seven or eight, who have virtually no means to defend themselves, such criminals are demonstrating the need for stronger punishment to a similar extent as other brutal felonies. In other words, sex offenders against children are absolutely and completely exploiting defenseless entities for no particular, reasonable reason except to fulfill their own desires.

Another reason why I believe sex crimes are quite different from other crimes such as burglary or fraud is that sex crimes utterly crush the victim's most basic and fundamental right and dignity—namely, the right over one's own body. In most cases, sex crimes not only crush the victim's right over his/her body, but they also crush and murder the soul. The experience becomes a trauma that is hard—if not impossible—to forget for the rest of the child's life. The victims not only experience trauma from the unforgettable pain and terror of the crime, but also—especially in the cases of young child victims—frequently turn the cause and fault of the crime back to themselves and become traumatized about their entire lives.

Those who argue against the harsh punishment toward child sex offenders talk about the rights of the criminals, pointing to the fact that South Korea must remain a democratic, human-rights-upholding nation. However, when the seven-year-old victim of the Naju child rape incident is still terrified by the gruesome reality she must face after her surgery and the offender lies in his cell, eats his lunch, watches baseball, and then reads fantasy novels, whose human rights are we genuinely arguing for? I personally believe that in this situation—irrelevant to the discussion of human rights—the criminal justice system (a crucial quality of a democratic nation) is malfunctioning and not doing its job. The fundamental reason why we have a criminal justice system is to punish criminals, achieve justice, and prevent further crimes. Although there are also purposes such as rehabilitation, when the offenders have the wrong mindset that they can just go and live a few years in prison while the family members of the victim are jumping up and down in agony, it seems that we are putting the cart before the horse.

In America, a sex offender who raped a teenager recently received a sentence of 99 years, amounting to penal service for life. Several European countries including Germany and Norway have already been implementing physical/chemical castration as punishment methods for sex offenders against children. It is regretful to observe that Korea, an equally democratic country, gives out sentences of 3 to 5 years in prison to those who crush the rights of children under 13 if they claim that they were intoxicated during the act.

When dealing with sex crimes, we cannot follow the simple dichotomy of the direct victim and direct offender. We must think of the entire nation as a victim to the crime. That is, we must consider the fact that sex crimes in particular tend to restrict the right to feel secure of every parent, child, and student in this nation. As a senior high school student in South Korea, I should be busily studying for exams and reading books in order to enter the university. However, whenever we hear about crimes such as the Naju child rape, we have no choice but to let go of our pens and look up from our books because we are genuinely horrified and saddened by the dark side of society we are so busily preparing to jump into. According to an article in *Hankuk Ilbo* (2012/09/01), almost half of all sex crimes against children and teenagers are committed by people acquainted with the victims. Thus, whenever such incidents occur, it is not a stretch to say that people lose some faith in those who closest to them—our teachers, our neighbors, perhaps even our family members. It is not an exaggeration to say that sex crimes contribute to the collapse of our social fabric. Thus, such crimes are not detached from anyone; they are extremely relevant to every member of our society.

However, what is as important as establishing a principle, philosophical foundation for the argument of stronger punishment is actually having a more practical plan and taking action. Ultimately, in order to have harsher penalties for the criminals, we have to change the legislation. One of the biggest problems in Korea is the large perception and consciousness gap between those who work in the judiciary and the general public. Although the public's outcry for stronger penalties has consistently increased recently, the proportion of sex offenders receiving probation (or a suspended sentence) has actually increased. Thus, one necessary solution would be to introduce methods to reflect more of the 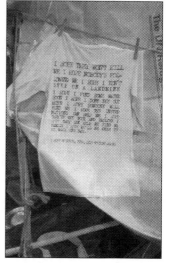 general public's view in the process of the law. Some methods could be open trials or public participation trials.

A few days ago, our school held a mock trial competition, and I was granted the rare opportunity to sit in the chief justice's chair and act as the judge in the trial. Before I went to sit in that position, I thought it would be simply an exciting experience to be in such a dignified and majestic spot. However, once I actually tried to judge the verdict of the first trial, I realized that the position was not as "cool" as I thought it would be; it was actually an extremely difficult position to be in due to the realization that so many people would be affected by my decision. Suddenly, the high seat I sat upon seemed not so majestic, but in fact quite precarious. In fact, I felt that it might be better for the judiciary system as well if it could gain more public support and legitimacy by introducing methods that could be more open to general public opinion. Instead of always being in the higher position, I felt that the judiciary system should sometimes actively strive to be not as far away and detached from the people it serves.

The issue of sex crimes against children is complex and touches upon so many aspects of human rights that it seems difficult to establish a definite opinion about it. Unquestionably, we must reflect our emotions, but the method and direction we take in order to reflect such feelings must not be temporary and overly emotional. Instead, it must be rational and calm, but constantly ongoing and unwavering. I hope that Korea can find an appropriate equilibrium between unbearable fury and level-headed rationality and seek for a wise solution to prevent any more similar crimes that trample upon some of our most vulnerable members' basic rights.

DO WE LOSE RIGHTS AS WE AGE?: CONFUCIUS ADDRESSES ELDER ABUSE

A common and typical perception about elders in Asian countries is that they are highly respected due to the relatively rigid hierarchy and social structure. Korea in particular was called as the "Eastern land of Courtesy" for its great emphasis on courtesy toward our older citizens. However, regretfully, there has been an increasing amount of elder abuse in Korea recently. Several incidents in which elderly citizens have been verbally or physically assaulted in the subway have caused great controversy. This essay examines this issue from the lenses of Confucius and his idea about respecting the elderly.

All human beings grow old. We accept this as a natural and ubiquitous procedure of life. In the majority of cases, people are granted more rights as they age—not only the legally stipulated rights, but also those that are implicitly agreed upon by society. To illustrate, parents tend to give more freedom to teenagers than to toddlers. Adults make more independent decisions than teenagers do. The fact that our society grants a wider capacity and broader domain to older people is, to a certain extent, an acknowledgment that age means more experience and knowledge to be a more rational and responsible citizen. If this is true, it seems that the 21st century has confronted a strange contradiction.

Despite the increasing age expectancy attributed to medical and technological improvements, a vast majority of senior citizens in Korea suffer from elder abuse. Uncountable cases are reported of people over 65 being injured, mistreated, or exploited. A horrendous number of them have no job, family, or financial support by the government. Indifferent negligence is rampant; we frequently hear the news of elderly people committing suicide and their cold bodies being discovered by their neighbors weeks later. More moderate examples are those of discrimination, such as when the elderly are rejected from health insurance or healthcare facilities due to their frequent illnesses. In Korea, where it is the tradition for the son to provide for his aged parents, the most unbearable part of being old is the lack of dignity and self-consciousness in being a burden to the rest of the family. It is undoubtedly clear that raising awareness about elder abuse and doing away with it brick by brick is an imminent task that can no longer be pushed aside.

In this essay I hope to shed light on this issue by looking over some applicable ideas of the philosopher Confucius, who still acts as an overarching influence in many Asian nations.

Throughout his life, Confucius (551-479 BCE) placed a unique emphasis on human relationships. As a philosopher of the "Spring and Autumn period," he believed that the disorder and brutality of his days could be solved by rightly establishing human relationships amongst members of the society. Confucius explained that the underlying principle when interacting with another person should be the value of ren—the way of virtue, morality, compassion and love. This view is well represented by Confucius' Golden Rule of Being, which requires that we "treat others only as you consent to being treated in the same situation." Confucius deemed loving others as a "calling and mission for which one should be ready to die" (Lunye 15.9), which demonstrates the weight he placed on such ideas.

Based on the foundation of universal compassion for others, Confucius further delineated the distinctive relationships that exist among people. He argued that, in such relationships, there must be Li in order for ideal social order to be achieved. Li indicated the actual rituals for how people should act according to the decrees of propriety. Thus, Confucius believed in the necessity for people to abide by a certain rule of conduct and the external expression of such procedures. More importantly, Confucius underscored that such routines should not be perfunctory; they must be internalized and deeply imbedded within society in order to attain genuine harmony. Amongst the five relationships he demarcates, there are the relationships between the elder to junior and the father to son. The Li required from the younger entity is deference and filial piety. Thus, one must not only show physical politeness and fraternal submission, but also sincere respect and reverence toward the elderly.

The question that must be asked and answered in depth at this point is why does elder abuse happen at the fundamental level? Although various factors are involved, I will focus specifically on the aspect of education. Nowadays, education on the righteous attitude toward the elderly does not happen through tangible subjects and textbooks taught at school. Such lessons are mostly conveyed and displayed by the values upon which a society stands. In many East Asian countries, including Korea, Confucianism has been a major long-lasting influence on every aspect of daily life. In other words, Confucianism is deeply imbedded in their value systems. Yet elder abuse is equally, if not more so, a serious issue for the East and West alike. So does this indicate the failure of Confucius' education?

I say no. Confucius' meaning of education was not just the lectures he taught to students that have been passed along through books. The passive transfer of information was only the first step of teaching and learning; the authentic sense of education came when one truly understood the matter by heart and extended such comprehension to action. Confucius' thoughts on education are demonstrated through his famous words, "He who learns but does not think is lost." One must not only listen to lectures, but also think and deliberate deeply upon what he or she learned, appreciating it fully to the point at which the lesson could be carried out through action.

Thus, elder abuse is so prevalent even in "Confucian countries" because the new generation knows but does not understand the need to respect our seniors. The majority know by theory and principle that the elderly should be respected. Regardless, elder abuse is committed by those who have failed to identify with and apply such knowledge in their actions. Why do these people fail to fully understand such a straightforward idea? One reason could be the frustration and confusion coming from the lack of consistency between Confucius' lessons and the trend of the modern day. It is understandable that fraternal submission or unconditional filial piety does not tend to fit in today's shift toward less family values and more focus on the independent individual. Another reason could be the heightened emphasis on superficial appearance; people are increasingly putting more value on looks and physical qualifications. There is a burgeoning will to look beautiful, handsome, and young, as demonstrated by the unprecedented cosmetic surgery boom in various nations. There is also a perception that creativity—a quality highly valued in the 21st century—somehow comes from young age and deteriorates as we grow older. In such a social atmosphere, it is almost predictable—with few exceptions—that the elderly are pushed to the side and degraded. In contrast, in Confucius' day, age itself was viewed as a great fortune and it was a common belief that people ripen and blossom in their wisdom through aging. Confucius himself mentioned that a good teacher was "someone older who is familiar with the ways of the past and the practices of the ancients."

I believe that one way we can relieve the disparity between lectures and the reality and overcome our amplified fixation on appearances is through education. That is, we must take a different route in education. If we observe countries that rank relatively high on the happiness and equality index of the elderly, they do not enforce a vertical social structure in which the young must unconditionally be submissive to the old. Rather, the youth and the elderly are more like friends and neighbors, respecting one another as fellow citizens who have equal rights and responsibilities. Adapting such an approach in education could be a fresh change and a possible solution to the issue of elder abuse nowadays.

A Right to a "Happy" Education

In October of 2012, a Korean high school senior reads the different types of fundamental rights granted by the Constitution. Equality in front of the law, the right to own property, the right to work . . . and "the right to education."

It is not a far stretch to say that senior year in high school is when studying becomes most precious. Entrance exams and college applications lay straight ahead, and there is no other time when studying is so important. However quite ironically, the Korean high school senior who reads the Constitution stops abruptly at the phrase that says "Every person has the right to receive education." She likely lets out a frustrated sigh, while responding. "Okay, okay. I get it. Studying is important." She reluctantly admits the truth of her situation. And although she and her friends place a small timer on their desks to measure the time they study each day and make joint promises to "study harder and use time wisely," at a certain point, the most desperate right that high school seniors in Korea identify with becomes not "the right to education" but rather "the right to the pursuit of happiness." In today's world it feels like 'studying' and 'education' are not fundamental and basic rights but more like fundamental, basic obligations. So today in response and perhaps as a declaration of sorts I decided not to open my textbook and study, but instead open my laptop and write a truly honest story about my thoughts on living as a senior student in Korea.

I do not think negatively about Korea's well known and unique passion for education. In fact, I believe that huge emphasis on education and human resources is the reason for Korea's rapid development into a major economic power in the last half of the 20th century. However for education to be a truly persistent and constant driving force instead of merely a temporary stimulus, I say that we must take a step back, ponder, and think carefully about how our education has been delivered and gained and how it should be in the future.

I feel a major problem with the current education environment in Korea is that students are not fully conscious of their 'right' to education. That is, students to do not view education as something they should actively claim and demand. Students instead think that just because they are sitting in front of a blackboard and listening to a lecture, their 'right to education' is automatically fulfilled. I think it is time for students to change that mindset; they should acknowledge the truth that they have an active right to a 'happy education' and an education that pertains to and honors basic student rights. 'Happiness' is a feeling that appears in us when we strive toward a goal we truly regard as valued personally. A majority of students in Korea feel that they are 'unhappy' and number one reason for student deaths in Korea is not an illness, but suicide. The reason? A lot of these students do not genuinely 'value' the education they are receiving or do not know why they are receiving it. Rather they think it is simply a reality that they must accept. However, the right to education should not be seen as a passive right but rather an active right that is worthwhile and valuable for them individually.

What we need in order to achieve that "happy" education is not just a change in students' thoughts, but also an organic shift in the approach those in Korea take to educate students. The suggestion I would make is that we should work to achieve 'student rights' through 'education' because a happy education can only happen when we do not sacrifice fundamental student rights just to educate our children and make them study. A circumstance that has been consistently criticized in Korea is that students study so hard; they do not have the freedom to breathe. They wake up early and study until midnight, and after school, a private academy always awaits them. This is the inconvenient and uncomfortable truth for too many students in Korea.

So currently, there are substantive movements toward achieving real 'student rights.' For example, several cities and provinces have created 'student right ordinances' and are implementing them in their schools. These ordinances grant more freedom to students in spheres where freedom was previously limited. Students are such granted rights as the right to assemble, the right over one's body (corporal punishment or any other type of mental / physical punishment is not allowed), the right to express one's individuality, and several others.

As a teenager and a student, I view these changes as a positive shift. However there are many who argue against these new ordinances, saying that this sudden implementation of a new policy has caused students to become rude and lawless, even to the extent they are ignoring their teachers. After the implementation of the ordinances, there was a great deal of controversial news reports about students becoming more violent and teachers' struggling to keep order in their classrooms.

I would cautiously respond, however, it is quite unfair to say that these new student rights ordinances are the direct cause of more "lawless" students. It seems more right to say that if, until now, we could silence students through the restriction of their rights or delivering undue and harsh punishments, after the implementation of the ordinances, the voices of previously overly silenced students are simply seeping out, glad to be heard at least. I have been reading a book recently, called "Student rights questions Education," where the author declares that now is a time when 'maturation' can happen through 'chaos.' What we need is not another, new alternative to keep students obedient and silent, but rather a more fundamental change that can help students feel both more respected and more responsible in and out of their classrooms.

I believe a more fundamental change should come, starting with what students do most—get an education. We should thoroughly examine how students are being educated and try to find a way to make that method more consistent with our human rights values. Giving more discretion and freedom to students to choose their hairstyles and clothes is a positive direction, but that should not be the only and law way we try to protect student rights.

The primary method of teaching in Korea is frequently described as "teaching by rote." That is, teachers give a one-sided lecture, students write down lecture notes, they memorize the material, and take a test based on their memorization and comprehension skills. I do not completely discount the importance of such teaching methods. In many cases, the method can be the most efficient and maybe even the most necessary way to proceed. However what I further propose is that there should be a new balance between such traditional methods of teaching and new methods that listen to and demand more students' voices.

I believe the most crucial element to respecting any person or group's rights, is to acknowledge that person/group as an equal entity on an equal footing. An over-focus on "teaching by rote" implies, although may not directly intend, that students are not mature, not equal as adults and thus, they must listen and memorize and never express and think. I do admit as well that the majority of students are not as mature as fully fledged adults, which is why society ban certain things (e.g. tobacco, alcohol, etc.) until we become adults. However I simultaneously content there is never a justification to ban students' "free and open thinking." Every being should be allowed to express their thoughts freely, as long as their thoughts are not clearly harmful to another individual or society. However in an educational environment

that puts a heavy, heavy emphasis on rote memorization of skills and facts, it is not a stretch to argue that one of the most fundamental rights of students is ignored or restricted, whether directly or indirectly.

To become a bit more personal, ever since I started to debate, I have changed in many ways. I realized that one of the major changes in my thinking is that I have become much more active in pursuing my rights. That is, I have learned that critical thinking is not an instance of being 'rude' or contrary to the Asian value of 'modesty,' but is something I can and should exercise freely. From the basic fact that I can freely think in different directions, even in a direction that contradicts my teacher's thinking, I now realize the importance of 'questioning' what I previously accepted without any doubts. I believe this active attitude is the most important step toward achieving any type of human rights. It is our 'right'—we should be the ones actively claiming for them and evaluating them.

When I teach debate to young elementary students every Saturday, we start with easy motions related to school. In the first class, we started to talk about the topic, "Should students wear school uniforms." When the three young girls could not think of an argument, I asked them, "Why do you think the school makes us wear uniforms in the first place?" The three looked up at me and were suddenly lost in thought. They tilted their heads and replied, "You're right. Why do we wear uniforms, anyway?" Their inquiry developed into a fruitful, critical, and rational discussion that simple lectures on the topic likely would have failed to provide.

Some people are concerned that more active students will only create a situation where students become full of them and do not respect others, including their peers, teachers, and parents. However the other side of the coin of rights is responsibility. When students realize the significance and importance of rights, they will also realize and recognize that others have exactly the same rights as they do. When we debate, therefore, we do not just speak and assert our own views; we have the obligation and thus the incentive to listen to our opponent and partner, and address the judge.

The main reason why there is bullying and violence in schools is because most bullies do not realize the simple fact that their victims have basic fundamental rights, indeed the same rights as they do. But also, it is because bullies do not realize the fact that they also must take on responsibility. The whole concept of my own and others' rights has become today more of an intangible, a something-in-the-far-future idea for many students. The solution is to make students learn they have exercisable, tangible rights, and steer our direction toward teaching them that their rights pertain and extend to others as well.

If, until now, Gangnam-style education focused on rapidly filling students with what we think they should know, the style of education should move more towards helping students expand their thoughts out into the classroom. The step toward understanding one's genuine 'right to education' comes with individual realization that 'the right to education' ultimately exists within the big picture of better overall 'student rights.'

LET TEENS DREAM FOR AN IDEAL

T his essay was written after watching the movie "Splendid Holiday" during class. "Splendid Holiday" was the unofficial military operation name for the martial law imposed on May 18, 1980, when citizens of Gwangju rose up against the military government in the Gwangju democratization movement to fight a bloody battle for democracy. The movie is recognized as a visage of Korea's painstaking and desperate efforts to achieve democracy.

Whenever my father drives me to school, he turns on songs from the 1970s and 1980s. One day, rolling down the window and taking in the fresh air of Ga-pyeong city, we joyfully sang Kim Hak Lae's classic "If I were a speechless wanderer." When Kim Min Ki's song "Road" came on the radio, we were both speechless. My father seemed to look serious and even a bit sad. Looking into his eyes, I felt strangely solemn too.

> "Various roads . . . But who says this is the only one . . ."
> "Various roads . . . The road we will meet at least once more before we die . . ."

When my father first told me that this song, which was illegal during his university years, contains the aspirations and hopes for democracy, I had mixed feelings. Since a certain point in history, the word *democracy* has naturally held a positive connotation. With such emotion, I closed my eyes and carefully listened to the song again, but I could not receive as deep an impression as my father. Eventually, I got bored with the repetitive melody and asked my dad to turn on a new song.

I was finally able to understand why my father loved songs that dealt with Korea's past democratic movement after I watched the movie "Splendid Holiday" for the third time. To those who had been part of the bloody uprising against the former military government in 1980, the desperate fight and ardent desire for democracy were not just sporadic, typhonic emotions that faded away into history. I then realized that, to my father, who had been part of the active demonstrations in his university years, the fight for democracy was being erased into a simple memory. Compared to that unforgettable historical fight for democracy, it felt as if we now gave permission to forget the past too easily. Although we were all speechless and cried while watching the movie, afterwards I observed my classmates turning on the light and turning off the screen. At that moment, they were already worrying about next period's pop quiz. Feeling that I too might forget this deep impression I felt while watching the movie, I put on my headphones and started to write down my feelings while listening to Kim Min Ki's "Road."

We call a person who devotes his/her life to something bigger than himself/herself a hero. In that sense, the characters in the movie who sacrificed everything to fight for democracy were, indeed, heroes. Looking at those who willingly jumped into the bloody fight against the military government and subsequently looking at ourselves—fighting ferociously against our test scores in order to get into college—made me feel an emptiness that was hard to describe with words.

Maybe we were devoting our lives to something too small.

It suddenly felt like the pop quiz scores, the final test and applications that we fought so eagerly to protect were not things that were truly bigger than us. If we did not dedicate our lives to some bigger ideal after we graduated (or at least during some phase in our life), looking back at our lives, we would feel that same emptiness and sadness.

In that sense, after watching "Splendid Holiday" I became thankful of the fact that during my freshmen years when I was full of novel dreams, instead of only filling myself with knowledge, I had promised myself to live for a bigger ideal. My ideal and my dream are to help make a world in which every person—regardless of ethnicity, gender, economic status, or any other external status—is granted the most fundamental rights and dignity as a human being.

The event that made me really think about the concept of human rights occurred in Cambodia, where I went for volunteer work. The old, deteriorating classroom in Siem Leap had more than 50 students crammed inside. While I was teaching them English, rain suddenly started to pour down from the sky and water ferociously splashed into the room. When the children rushed to shut the wooden windows and door, the room—having no electricity—became pitch black. I awkwardly stood in the darkness and listened to the raindrops slamming down on the roof. Suddenly, another sound grasped my attention. From a corner of the darkness, a boy, unaffected by the circumstances, bashfully but confidently said, "It's okay. Please teach."

It struck me then, that there was something much more profound about the boy's timid but resolute request. Amidst the blackness, he was asking not just for an English expression, but a basic right to the education to which he was righteously entitled. It felt like within the blackness of the world's negligence, the children were demanding something we were obliged to give: fundamental rights.

From then on, I felt that I lived my high school years while asking for a value that was greater than just my individual needs and wants. However, at several points, that dream was let down. One day, I was researching for a debate motion under the theme of religion and gender equality when I encountered a YouTube video of a woman charged with adultery being stoned to death in the middle of the road. Seeing a scene I had only read about in books materializing in front of my eyes through the video, I felt immensely solemn and gloomy. The townsmen in the video nonchalantly buried the woman's body halfway into the sand and surrounded her in a circle, throwing stones at her body and her face. When the woman fell to the ground with the facial expression of a person who hated everything about the world and a body bloody from the stones, the people surrounding her started to walk away as if nothing had happened.

It was a moment when I felt that the most important values of my life were collapsing. I realized that ensuring even just one individual's basic human rights required so much effort and energy, and now I understood that there was an enemy out there that could take away one person's entire life so easily. It was truly discouraging. In front of that enemy I felt immensely weak, and my dreams seemed like an ideal that could not be achieved in reality. Those moments of reality were a wake-up call for me to stop being so naïve. They felt like a preview moment of the real world to a teenager who had not yet stepped into the world completely.

Perhaps that was the reason why the movie "Splendid Holiday" made me cry so much. Although I have watched many other movies that were far sadder and more brutal, I had never felt the comparable heart-aching sting that "Splendid Holiday" made me feel all three times I watched it. The reason for this unique sadness was because, no matter how hard the characters in the movies fought for democracy, the enemies they faced were too ridiculously strong compared to them. Although the freedom fighters shook off their families' concerns and gathered at the city hall, they were killed easily and swiftly by the military.

The movie "Splendid Holiday" was uniquely sad because it showed how one individual's, one country's dream became "just a dream" in the cold brutality of reality. When Jin-woo, a high school student in the movie, leads his classmates to the demonstrations, I remember how the teachers stopped them in front of the school doors, saying "you don't know the world and the reality so you should go back indoors to study." Watching Jin-woo disobey his teacher's words and continuing to march to the demonstrations, some people might say that he is too full of brave but naïve spirit—especially considering the fact that he gets killed that day. However to me, the decision that Jin-woo made was especially touching.

Without the students and youth back in the 1980s, I believe that Korea might still be under a military government without the system of democracy that we have now. If the people back then had compromised with reality, I wonder how gloomily we would be living now. Although the ideal and dream that the youth fought for back then might have seemed hard to achieve and difficult to materialize, because they sacrificed everything for it, we can live in a better world today.

Thus, I do not want to abandon the dreams I had during my teens and during my 20s. I believe that every person has a certain social role and obligation, and I think that the most significant role of a teenager and youth is to dream and have an ideal bigger than themselves while maintaining the passion and spirit to protect that ideal.

Watching "Splendid Holiday" with my classmates, I felt that we—living happy lives and never having to directly confront the huge social unrest that happened in the 1980s—could very easily forget the ideals that we were chasing unless we continuously repeated and emphasized them to ourselves over and over again. Whenever I go to a debate tournament, the opponents I feel most bad for are those who speak without any kind of value and try to win the other side by providing a long laundry list of the realistic concerns and the numbers and statistics. On the other hand, I feel more touched by the debaters who—although they might not have the strongest logic or rhetoric— fight for a value and really try to protect it. If the teenagers who have not yet jumped into the climax of this brutal world do not dream, then who will? Although it may be a vague, indefinite plan, I believe that we need to dream of a society that we genuinely want in order to actually make a change and become the driving force to move toward that very society.

When I, quite adamantly and quite specifically, talk about my future goal to become a human rights lawyer, my parents become concerned. From time to time, they tell me that my dream of becoming a human rights lawyer might be just a naïve desire that I have when I am yet young and ignorant of the many realistic concerns. However, right now, I do not want to think about the so many practical and pragmatic concerns that I hear from my parents. Although such concerns are really concrete and significant, I do not want to abandon my dream because of them. I think the teenage years are too early to give up.

Teens, dream for an ideal.

I believe that is our right and our obligation.

PART V

HUMAN RIGHTS THROUGH EDUCATION

WHY IS EDUCATION THE ANSWER?

Millions of children worldwide must give up their right to live as an ordinary child in order to work every day to feed their family. Of course, the act of working as a child itself is not inherently bad. However, the severe problem of child labor does not surround the children who simply help out with a family business after school. It is an urgent and necessary concern for children as young as 5 who are forced to work in harmful conditions—including drug trafficking and sex work—for more than 20 hours a day, forgoing their basic right to receive any kind of education.

According to statistics provided by UNICEF, the problem of child labor is especially severe in Asia and Africa. Although this could be simply explained by the relatively higher rate of poverty in those nations, I believe the prevalence of child labor in a certain society can mean much more. Considering the direct correlation between the increase of child labor and the decrease of children receiving education, the pervasiveness of child labor could also imply that that society generally places a higher value on economic rights than on the right to an education. I do not think that all nations or communities place the same or at least similar values on education; for example, I heard that France considers being cultivated and educated as an utmost important quality of men and women alike, regardless of what kind of job the individual has.

After learning about the differing priorities the East and West place on rights (the Eastern view placing more emphasis on social, economic, and cultural rights while the Western view placing more emphasis on civil and political rights), I came to ponder upon a solution that could reduce the gap and balance out the differences. As an Asian myself, I especially focused on what could help enhance the importance of civil and political rights within Asia.

The conclusion I arrived at was education. It is not a stretch to say that education is a crucial part of achieving more political rights. Some people even say that an educated public is a prerequisite for a democracy. Put more simply, motivation for engaging in politics—whether it is passive or active participation—or motivation for fighting for rights such as the freedom of expression, peaceful assembly, and association comes far more easily when we have acquired general knowledge about the world and have cultivated the powers of reasoning and judgment. For this reason, throughout my high school years I focused on volunteer work that could genuinely provide a helpful education for children who most needed it.

Numerous economists and sociologists worldwide choose South Korea as their focus of study. They are particularly intrigued by how Korea, a nation that was one of the poorest in the world in the 1950s, could reach the economic prosperity of today. They are even more interested in how Korea could establish a relatively stable and well-functioning democracy along with its economic development.

To date, many people have pointed to Korea's unique national characteristics of diligence. However, I believe that another important factor could be Korea's zeal for education. Korea's lack of natural resources led to an emphasis on human resources. Many Koreans place their highest value upon becoming educated. It is not unusual at all to see students studying well past midnight or going to countless private academies after school. Although there would be many other factors, I think the unique academic environment within Korea is definitely one of the reasons why Koreans were and are relatively more eager to protect their various civil and political rights. It is truly amazing to see how, every time a major demonstration against a political issue is held, tens of thousands of people—with a huge portion of the people being students—gather to participate in the famous candlelight vigils.

As an addition to this discussion, although education has been one of the reasons why Korea has been able to achieve both rapid economic growth and democratic procedures, I should point out that that education might become one of the greatest problems this nation has to solve in the future. Much more effort is required to provide education that truly nurtures students' ability to think critically and creatively instead of cramming and memorizing knowledge for tests. Fortunately, there seems to be some positive changes especially from the  grassroots level, but there still needs to be a more influential shift of the paradigm that can accommodate a better quality education that genuinely helps everyone instead of a hurried education that only remembers the top 10%.

TACKLING THE DILEMMA
OF EDUCATION IN
DEVELOPING NATIONS

T he rain was falling lightly outside, seeping into the dry, parched land. Wiping the sweat from my eyebrows, I looked around at the fifty children before me. As I spoke slowly and wrote some words on the blackboard, I could hear the rain becoming heavier and louder. No more than five minutes had passed when clouds covered up the entire sky and the rain from above started to rattle down noisily on the plastic roof. When the water seeped into the classroom floors, I rushed to close the door. As the door shut behind me, the room darkened and I could only see the faint silhouettes of the children. The classroom had no lights; it had no windows let alone any artificial lighting. With no other option, I opened the door again, inviting more water and more noise from outside. Trying to act unaffected by the interruption, I resumed teaching the class the most common English expressions. When the sound from the storm drowned out my voice, the children would edge closer to me. They would lean over and stretch their necks to listen more carefully.

It was truly a scene that I will never forget. Working as a volunteer teacher in Cambodia during my summer vacation, I learned more from the students than I could possibly teach them. I learned that the darkness of the room and the cacophony of the rain could not discourage the children from their desire to learn.

The right to receive education is recognized as fundamental and is enshrined in Article 26 of the Universal Declaration of Human Rights. According to the declaration, everyone has a right to education that is "free, at least in the elementary and fundamental stages," while "technical and professional education shall be made generally available and higher education shall be equally accessible to all on the basis of merit." However, the status quo of free access to education is quite bleak, especially in developing nations, where nearly 2 billion children who do not receive proper education or any education at all. A study by the Global Fund for Children revealed that even amongst those who do receive some sort of education, one in five will not continue past the fifth grade.

The lack of education for children is a situation that all nations must attend to with a unique commitment and mandate. The reason for this emphasis is that deprivation of education is inevitably linked to additional problems that children confront, such as violence or poverty. Uneducated minors tend to lose an important opportunity to learn the necessary skills that will provide them competitiveness and economic independence.

Education is an investment; those who miss it are inherently in a position from which it is harder to earn a sustainable income. A recent study by the U.S. Bureau of Labor Statistics showed that people who finish higher education earned almost $175 more every week compared with those who dropped out. This resulting low income develops into a vicious cycle that is hard to overturn. Over time, the gap between the uneducated and educated expands and, in the long run, serves as a barrier that makes the uneducated systematically disenfranchised.

Not only do they earn less than the educated, but uneducated minors are also far more vulnerable to exploitation. It is not a coincidence that major social problems that children confront such as child labor or sex trafficking are crimes that are perpetuated by people who take advantage of the lack of knowledge of the uneducated or untrained children in rural, poor, or conflict-stricken regions. To end the prolongation of such circumstances, it is thus important for both developed and developing nations alike to take strong measures to provide access to primary and preferably even secondary and tertiary education for their children. In essence, "education is the primary vehicle by which economically and socially marginalized adults and children can lift themselves out of poverty" and create sustainable livelihoods.

The foremost step for tackling this problem is to grasp a better comprehension of why the lack of access happens in the first place. Although there can be various factors such as unique ethnic/cultural/gender prejudices or a lack of motivation for study, in this essay I plan to focus on specifically two reasons that generally have greater severity in both impact and extent: 1) the lack of incentive for the state to build schools or other educational institutions and necessary infrastructures and 2) although the infrastructure exists, children do not access them voluntarily/involuntarily due to external pressures.

An illustration of the former type would be children who have to walk for hours to reach a small school with inadequate teaching resources and bursting classrooms—a huge price to pay for unpromising returns. Naturally, children are gradually drawn away from the option of going to school and thus cannot fulfill their right to receive education. During my volunteer work in Cambodia, I witnessed this problem as students from remote rural areas faced considerable difficulties in reaching the school, which lacked classrooms, teachers, and educational materials.

The second type could be depicted by children who are forced into child labor or exploitative jobs to earn money. These children do not go to school because they themselves—or, in many cases, their parents—judge education to be less important than having immediate means for survival. For example, studies indicate that in Mexico almost 19 percent of children from 12 to 14 years of age work and not attend school. Similarly in Peru, only a third of all working children and adolescents aged six to 17 years attend school.

This is a group of children in which that the international community must be particularly interested and urgently address as these children are not only deprived of their right to education, but are also—in the majority of instances—going through additional human rights abuse during the exploitation and rigorous labor work. Child labor is, by definition, "labor that is performed by a child who is under the minimum age specified for that kind of work" which "jeopardizes the physical, mental or moral well-being of a child, because of its nature or because of the conditions in which it is carried out." Its worst forms can take place as slavery, trafficking, prostitution, debt bondage, and other forms of forced labor.

Child labor is closely intertwined with the broader problem of the lack of access to education as it is both a cause and effect of children unable to receive education. This is another global crisis confronting children that we have a mandate to address; the UNICEF reports that an estimated 250 million children aged 5 to 14 are still in child labor worldwide and the  United Nations states in article 32 of the "Convention on the Rights of Child" that children should be protected from economic exploitation. Despite the magnitude and severity of the issue, the lack of legislature regulating child labor and the lack of willingness to stop the abusive procedures create situations in which children cannot escape from the vicious cycle and consequently cannot enter into the educational realm they need.

Following the observation of the two broad groups, there must be realistic solutions that have feasibility and the high possibility of successful solvency. In the instance of the former group of children, it is most important to present a clear incentive for the state itself and motivate both the government and the private sector to allocate more resources for education. In other words, the approach is relatively top-down. This can be done by extending and expanding the role of a school or an educational institution.

The school would not simply function as a building in which students learn during the daytime, but would have multiple functions that ultimately better the community. In the status quo, many developed countries are increasingly implementing programs in rural communities in which the school can function as a cultural center for the town and provide a variety of social activities for not only children, but also adults. This trend can be adapted in less developed nations by the schools becoming institutions that serve as access points and converging sites. Having a set, secure facility in the center of a community can be immensely helpful for non-governmental organizations or even the government to implement social welfare programs. This is especially significant when we consider that one of the major reasons why both internal and external help could not benefit the people was that they were too dispersed and scattered in the region, which hindered the establishment of a systematic, sustainable, and organized form of assistance.

To illustrate, after the United Nations vigorously engaged in its mission of millennium goals, one of which was providing universal primary education, many schools were built in impoverished or ostracized places. Through such schools, students not only received education, but also a variety of social services. In Cambodia for example, UNICEF aid workers were able to provide school supplies, clothes, and clean water via the primary education institutions. Likewise, expanding the role a school can play in the community will bring additional incentives for the state to provide more infrastructures.

The second pattern of the problem should be addressed in a slightly different matter. For those children, it is more important to take a grassroots approach and incentivize the children and the families themselves to attend school and receive an education. The best way to create this incentive would be by making the schools provide immediate means of survival to the children. Commendable models would be Brazil's "Bolsa Escola" program, which focuses on providing financial aid for school attendance, or Egypt's program in which the Ministry of Education provides a meal to children during the school day as an incentive to attend school. More fundamentally, schools could have accommodating curriculums that can provide children with more pragmatic knowledge as well.

For example, the World Food program provided important nutrition education through schools that directly advantaged the children and their families through health benefits. "Back-to-School" programs incorporated agricultural productivity lessons for the numerous children who worked on farms. In addition, to tackle the dilemma of children choosing between labor and education, schools can have flexible schedules with different time slots that enable those students to consider multiple options.

In the case of Guatemala, since 1997 the government has been practicing flexible school-day programs that enable primary school children who spend the early morning hours working on farms to begin school later in the day. Although these innovative changes seem far-fetched and budget-constraining, they are not so infeasible when we consider the international trend of both developing and developed nations increasing investment in primary education. Vietnam's substantial increase of its national budget-spending on primary education from 7% to 20% or Ethiopia and Bangladesh initiating more proactive government policies on education are all examples that serve as evidence for this positive global trend.

Finding realistic ways to bring students back to school is more than just a pivotal task; it is an obligation, and one battle we cannot afford to lose. Education is a tool of self-defense for the generations of children who will otherwise not be given the adequate chance to break the cycle of poverty and exploitation they face. It is most efficient and effective to educate children and thus tackle the root cause of so many more challenges—one of them being the issue of child labor discussed herein. Personally, I have felt a strong determination to address these problems ever since I looked into the eager eyes of the Cambodian children and witnessed the potential for empowerment that education brings. Like Nelson Mandela correctly stated, "education is the most powerful weapon which you can use to change the world." Put education first, overcome the most urgent crisis, and change the world.

Personal Recount: A Week to Remember

Last summer vacation, I spent my time in Siem Leap, Cambodia doing volunteer work. Before leaving, my father told me that Cambodia is not just an exotic Southeast Asian country with rich tropical fruits. He told me with a grim expression that the "Killing Fields" is not just some urban legend. Cambodia's history includes a bloody phase in which a few individuals' radical ideals led to the massacre of more than a third of the population. The sadder part of this story is that it does not have an ending. Cambodia in its present day is still struggling from its lack of an educated population—the people who were killed mercilessly during the "Killing Fields" ages.

On the first day, we went to a place called Dail Organization. It was an institution that gave out lunch for people who had no money to afford any food. We made bread, rice, and other side dishes. After cooking, I served the food to the 400 people who had gathered at lunchtime. Most of them were young children, some hand in hand with their mothers or grandparents. One of the instructors at the institution explained that, for a majority of the people who came, the free lunch provided was the only food they could eat for the day. Looking at the children who smiled like little angels at the food they received, a strange sentiment swept over me. When the first serving had finished and there were still some rice left, the children ran over to me with plastic bags held in their hands. They stretched their arms out to attract my attention. These children wanted to take the leftover food to their families waiting for them back at home, whether it be their siblings or parents. Even when the leftover rice was all gone, there were many more children looking into my eyes desperately. I felt so bad that there was nothing I could do to help them that hot tears rolled down my cheeks. That day, almost all of the students from our school ate their dinner to the last grain of rice.

On the second, third, and fourth day in Cambodia, we went to a school for children from grades 1 to 9. We split into groups and went into different classrooms to teach the children English and paint the school. When our bus arrived on the school grounds, children rushed around our bus and jumped up and down to look inside. We stepped off the bus one by one, and the children stared at us with curious, deep eyes. When I waved at them, most of them broke into a big smile and waved back, while other more timid children ran away.

Our teacher assembled us and explained our schedule, but I couldn't really focus to listen to his words because I was captured by the children's eyes. The Cambodian children all had very big and beautiful eyes. They were deep and full, like a scoop of rich dark chocolate. They were twinkling with newly fueled curiosity and hope. As I looked into those eyes, I started to panic as I was pressed by the burden of having to meet the expectations of the children.

When our group met for the last time before we walked into the classrooms, the members were restless; one of the boys was suggesting that we didn't have to prepare so vigorously since we could easily improvise along the way. I felt the lack of motivation in some of our members, so I took a deep breath and started to talk. I asked them to think about the kids we saw on the Cambodian streets who followed us for half an hour, asking for money. A dollar or two could be virtually meaningless to many of our school students, but for many Cambodian kids, it was their lifeline for the day—as well as the lifeline of the 7, 8, or 9 more family members waiting at home. I told our group that, to these kids, perhaps our presence at this school for three days could be a truly crucial chance that doesn't come by any day.

To those kids, with such full expectations twinkling in their eyes, it would be blatantly and morally wrong to teach them with half-heartedness or inattentively. We had to pour in everything we had and try our very best to pass it on to these children. At the end of such a courageous attempt to motivate the others, I looked up and met the faces of my teammates. I was anxious because one of them still looked away dubiously. But I turned my head slowly to see the others and was delighted that they were nodding to my words.

After practicing more and rehearsing, we stepped into the classroom of 50 children. After introducing ourselves and singing a song together, our group started to teach the children as we had planned. But to our dismay, the gap in English proficiency amongst the children was too big. A  few students could write several English sentences with virtually no grammatical or spelling mistakes. Others did not even know the alphabet. In the first period, we were so confused and frustrated by the unexpected situation that we struggled to control the children and stumbled over our mess.

At break time, we stood nervously under the shade of a tree and talked about what we should do. Our conclusion was to first include many games and activities that all children—no matter how well they spoke or wrote English—could enjoy. We also agreed to divide our team into smaller groups in order to have deeper interpersonal conversations during the activities so that we could adjust to each individual's English level.

Instead of grammar or spelling, we focused on conversations that could be widely used in many different situations. We judged that the best we could do for the Cambodian students was to first make sure they felt more attachment to and at ease with English and then teach them the phrases they could actually apply in their daily lives. The pattern of teaching was to first do a 20-minute lecture of a certain subject, such as greetings, numbers, the weather, common verbs, or animals. After the lecture, we would play a related game or do a related activity for about 30 minutes. Using this method, all of the students could participate freely, and they seemed to enjoy the process of learning. We started off each period by asking the children questions using the expressions we had learned in the previous periods.

Standing in the position where I had to both plan and teach, I learned many valuable lessons that I could not have acquired from simply reading books. For example, when we played games with the children, I noticed that many other groups simply demonstrated or told the instructions and then directed the children to try for themselves. However I encouraged our group to play together for a change. Except for one or two members, we would sit amongst the children at their desks and play together. I felt that when we simply instructed the game or activity, it was as if we were in a higher or predominant position.

I thought the situation of us coming for volunteer work was clearly and inherently different from a normal lecture by a professor at school. Especially to young children, who are much more sensitive, the perception of a group of foreign students—only slightly older than them—coming to teach could hurt their feelings.

For the same reason, I tried to meet the eyes of the children by crouching down or lowered my body. Looking around, I was happy to see my other teammates doing the same. Such lessons, were not actually so grand and hard to realize. In fact, they came from simply having respect for the children. By respecting the children and embracing them as equally precious students as we are, I could simulate the situation in my mind by substituting myself instead of the Cambodian students. The question I constantly asked myself was "what would I feel like?"

After I could put myself in their shoes, I could truly be involved with them. I started to see details I could not see before. Having deeper conversations and closer observations, I noticed that the 50 or so students in the class were not all familiar with each other as we had assumed. The students came from all over the town, walking great distances to come to school. Although they sat together, some students did not even know their classmates' names.

Based on this observation, I organized an activity in which two students sitting together would draw each other's faces. The one rule of this activity was that the students could only look at the other student's eyes while drawing. As the students could not look down at the paper, the pictures turned out to be very funny. The great part was that students who usually hated drawing faces they thought they were not pretty or handsome did not mind this activity as every single picture in the room was just as bizarre. The Cambodian students were initially shy about doing the activity, but soon laughed and grinned at the pictures they had drawn.

After drawing the pictures, with our teams' help, the students asked their partners several questions regarding their names, ages, and hobbies. At the end of the activity, every student in the classroom had a mini profile of his or her partner. Afterwards, we asked the partners to come to the front of the class to introduce on another using the phrases "This is," "She likes," "He is," and so on.

When the weather was sunny, we could go outside to play various games as well. The Cambodian students were very used to running outside since there were not many means of entertainment. When we walked out of the classroom, my eyes met with those of a young girl. She looked down at my shoes, which were colorful and almost brand new. I looked at her feet and saw she had no shoes on. I felt so bad and started to hate my decision of wearing my favorite shoes to the school. I took off my shoes and felt my toes seep into the grass and mud beneath me. With bare feet I ran with the children or played ball with them. But while doing so I scraped my feet against some sharp rocks, which caused my feet to bleed. It hurt so much that I had to take painkillers. The teachers took me to the office and made me sit on a chair with my feet held high to stop the bleeding. I felt a bit ashamed that I was making such a fuss about my feet when I could be teaching the children back at the class. Although the teachers tried to persuade me not to go, I hopped backed to the classroom.

After the two days of teaching ended, I felt exhausted but glad. Our team had worked really hard, and our only hope was that the children had learned a lot from us during our stay. The next day, we arrived at the school once more to paint the school, which was old and had paint peeling off. We wiped the cobwebs off the windows and painted them with the hopeful color of bright blue. The walls were painted with the pure and clean color of light yellow, and one of our students painted beautiful pictures on them. The bright blue paint matched with the color of the sky above us.

After finishing with the painting, taking a deep breath of the air around me, I stepped out of the office to walk to the bus at the parking lot. At that moment, I was startled by the large group of students who were waiting in front of the office, calling out my name. They smiled shyly saying they wanted to take a photo with me. Although it was raining, we stood in front of the classrooms in the rain to take photos. When the children hugged me I felt my eyes filling up with tears. When a young girl ran over to me and kissed me on the cheek saying she loved me, I hugged her thin body tightly. The truly unbelievable marvel of these children was that they never stopped smiling. Those who didn't smile with their mouths did so with their twinkling eyes. They were so warm hearted and affectionate that I was overwhelmed by the love I received from them. In the rain, I wiped the tears of one of the children and held hands with another. Waving my hands to them, I was truly happy to be me.

As I trod up the winding stairs to my hotel room, I was confident that today was one of the most exhausting days of my life. When I reached the second floor, my friend walked over and handed me a letter, saying a kid from the school wanted me to have it. I managed a smile despite the tsunami of fatigue that swept over me. I unfolded the letter in front of my hotel door and read it, eyes wandering around the paper.

"You are the good people. I will always dream about you. Precious people like you are always remembered. I love you."

Walking numbly into the room, I sat on my bed and read the letter once more. I suddenly felt warm all over, and I looked back at the days behind me, trying to store as many memories as I could in my mind. During all these days, it seemed as if I had poured in everything I had to these children of Cambodia. I had given them all of my passion, energy, genuine love, and knowledge. Yet while I read the letter again and again, it became clear that I had received much more from these children. On the last day at the school, I remember that I was sitting in the library when the school principal teacher turned on an antique cassette tape next to me. The song was—to my surprise—"Ari-rang," a traditional Korean song. Looking at the principal teacher who was humming to the tune and feeling the cool breeze coming from the window, I felt that we were receiving more than we had given to this school and to Cambodia.

I had always had this perception of volunteer work in my conscience that people who volunteered felt more satisfied and proud of their good deeds. However, after my week in Cambodia, and after looking into the eyes of the children there, I learned that volunteer work actually made me feel more humble and even sorry to some extent, since what I had done for the past days seemed so inadequate compared to amount of help needed in the world in which we live. Why did the Cambodian children have to suffer in poverty while we were so blessed? Was it some sin that the Cambodian children committed and some grander deed that we managed to do? I learned that volunteer work is not an activity that people do when they have extra free time or when they need better reputations; rather, it is something we have to do when we are born luckier than our neighbors. It is not necessarily work, but sharing that is natural and beautiful.